THE GIANT SIGHT WORD WORKBOOK

T0088195

Diego Jourdan Pereira

THE GIANT SIGHT WORD WORKBOOK

Fun Activities for Kids Learning to Read and Write

300 HIGH-FREQUENCY WORDS!

FOR YOUNG READERS

To my goddaughter, Carmen Elena.
May she grow into a fine young writer
someday!

Copyright © 2021 by Diego Jourdan Pereira

All rights reserved. No part of this book may be reproduced in any manner without the express written consent of the publisher, except in the case of brief excerpts in critical reviews or articles. All inquiries should be addressed to Racehorse Publishing, 307 West 36th Street, 11th Floor, New York, NY 10018.

Racehorse for Young Readers™ books may be purchased in bulk at special discounts for sales promotion, corporate gifts, fund-raising, or educational purposes. Special editions can also be created to specifications. For details, contact the Special Sales Department, Skyhorse Publishing, 307 West 36th Street, 11th Floor, New York, NY 10018 or info@skyhorsepublishing.com.

Racehorse for Young Readers™ is a pending trademark of Skyhorse Publishing, Inc.®, a Delaware corporation.

Visit our website at www.skyhorsepublishing.com.

10 9 8 7 6 5 4 3 2 1

Library of Congress Cataloging-in-Publication Data is available on file.

Cover and interior design by Diego Jourdan Pereira

Mechanical design by Kai Texel

Dot to Dot font designed by A New Machine at MyFonts.com. Used under license.

Fredoka One and Fredoka dingbats open fonts designed by Milena Brandao at FontSquirrel.com.

ISBN: 978-1-63158-673-6

Printed in China

A B C D E F G H I J K L M N O P Q R S T U V W X Y Z

CAN YOU WRITE THE LETTERS BY YOURSELF?

WRITE AND LEARN THE SIGHT WORDS.

and and and and

and

are are are are

are

and and and

and

A B C D E F G H I J K L M N O P Q R S T U V W X Y Z

It may be small but works very hard. What is it?

ant ant ant

ant

ask ask ask

ask

One a day keeps the doctor away. What is it?

apple apple

apple

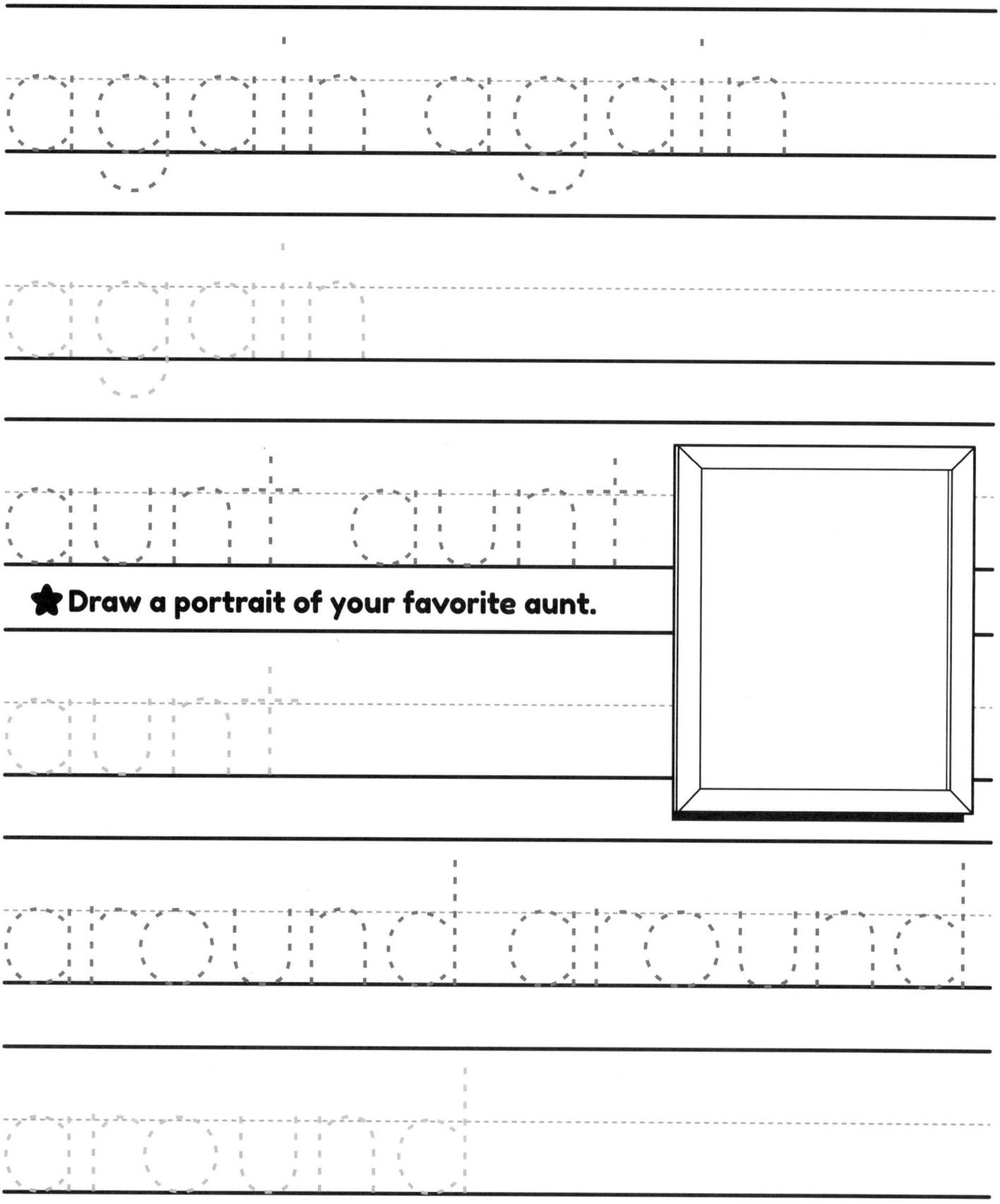
Draw a portrait of your favorite aunt.

above above

above

always always

always

answer answer

answer

TRACE, WRITE, AND COLOR!

Last April the little apple seed grew into a tall apple tree.

A B C D E F G H I J K L M N O P Q R S T U V W X Y Z

CAN YOU WRITE THE LETTERS BY YOURSELF?

WRITE AND LEARN THE SIGHT WORDS.

be be be be

be

big big big big

big

ball ball ball

Color it blue.

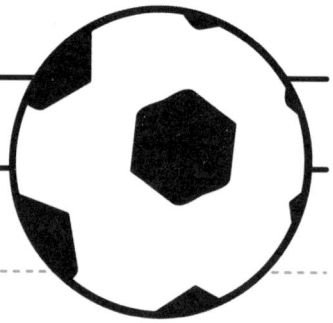

ball

bee bee bee

★ **Trace the bee's path to the flower.**

bee

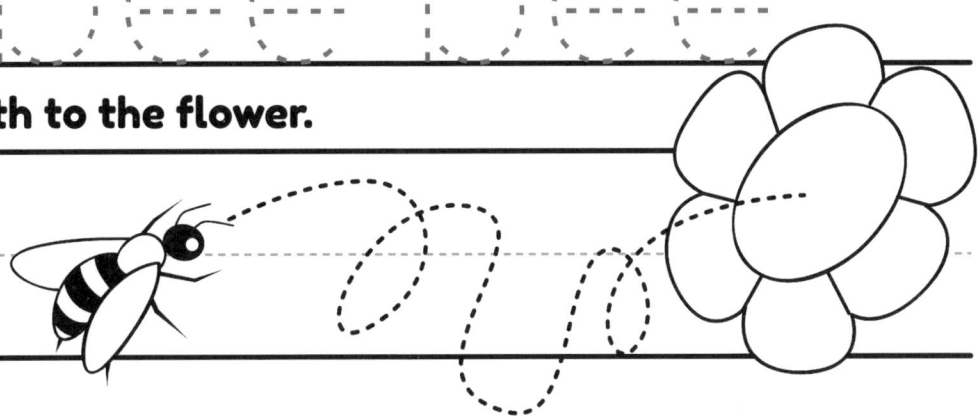

blue blue blue

blue

bird bird bird

bird

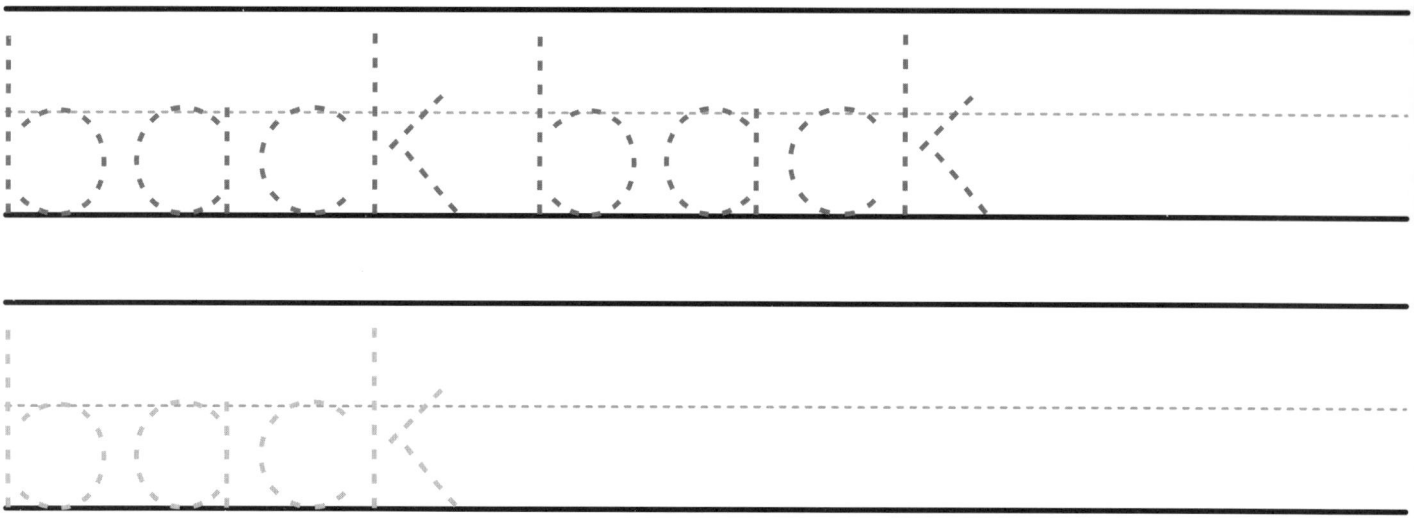

★ **Trace the dots to finish the drawing.**

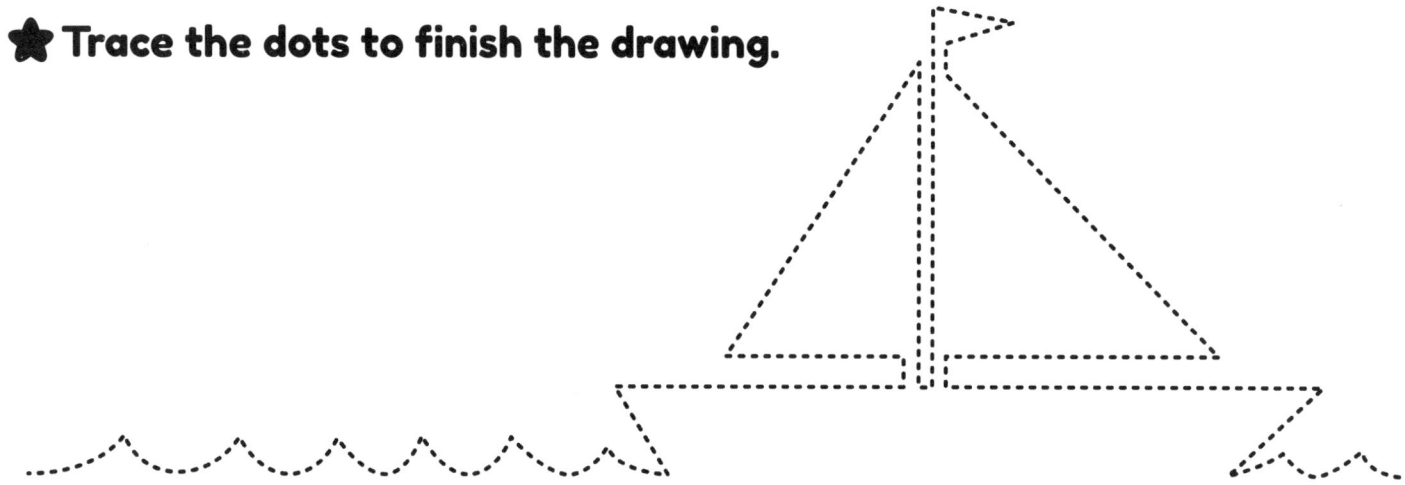

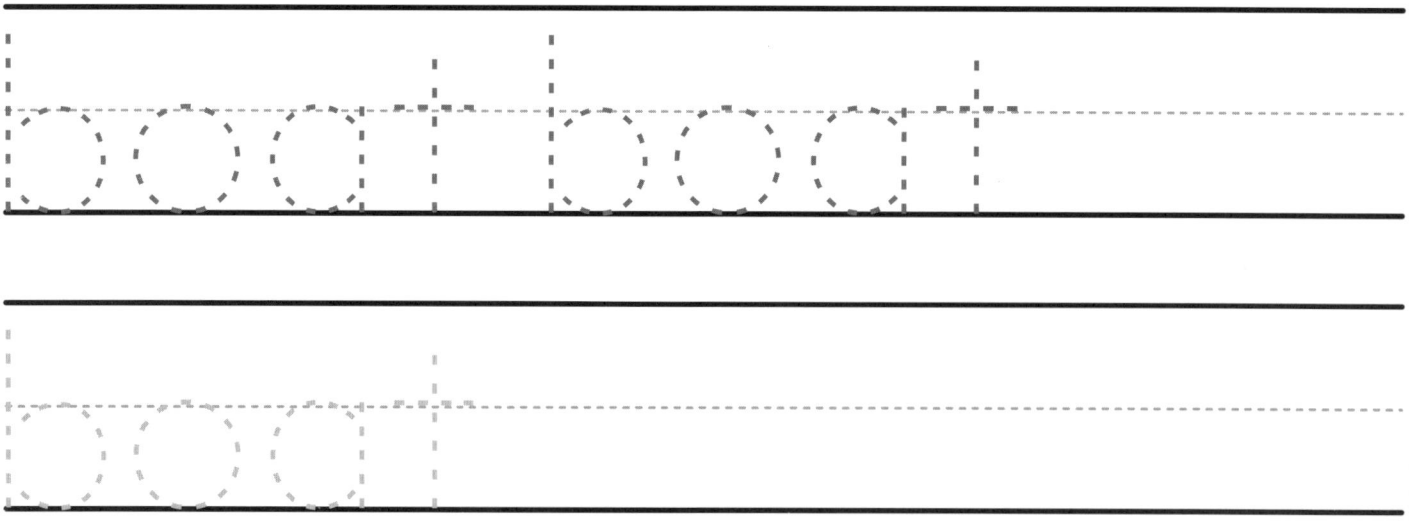

below below

below

both both

both

begin begin

begin

TRACE, WRITE, AND COLOR!

CAN YOU WRITE THE LETTERS BY YOURSELF?

WRITE AND LEARN THE SIGHT WORDS.

cat cat cat

cat

cat cat cat

cat

Draw the cat in three easy steps.

car car car

car

cow cow cow

cow

cone cone

cone

cake cake cake

cake

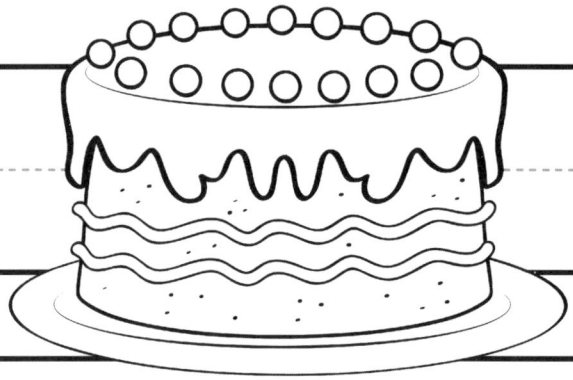

color color

How many colors do you know?

color

city city

city

close close

close

close close

close

★ **Color the flag red, white, and blue.**

country

country

★ **TRACE, WRITE, AND COLOR!**

Most city cats

love to chase

mice but these

two

are

close friends.

A B C **D** E F G H I J K L M N O P Q R S T U V W X Y Z

CAN YOU WRITE THE LETTERS BY YOURSELF?

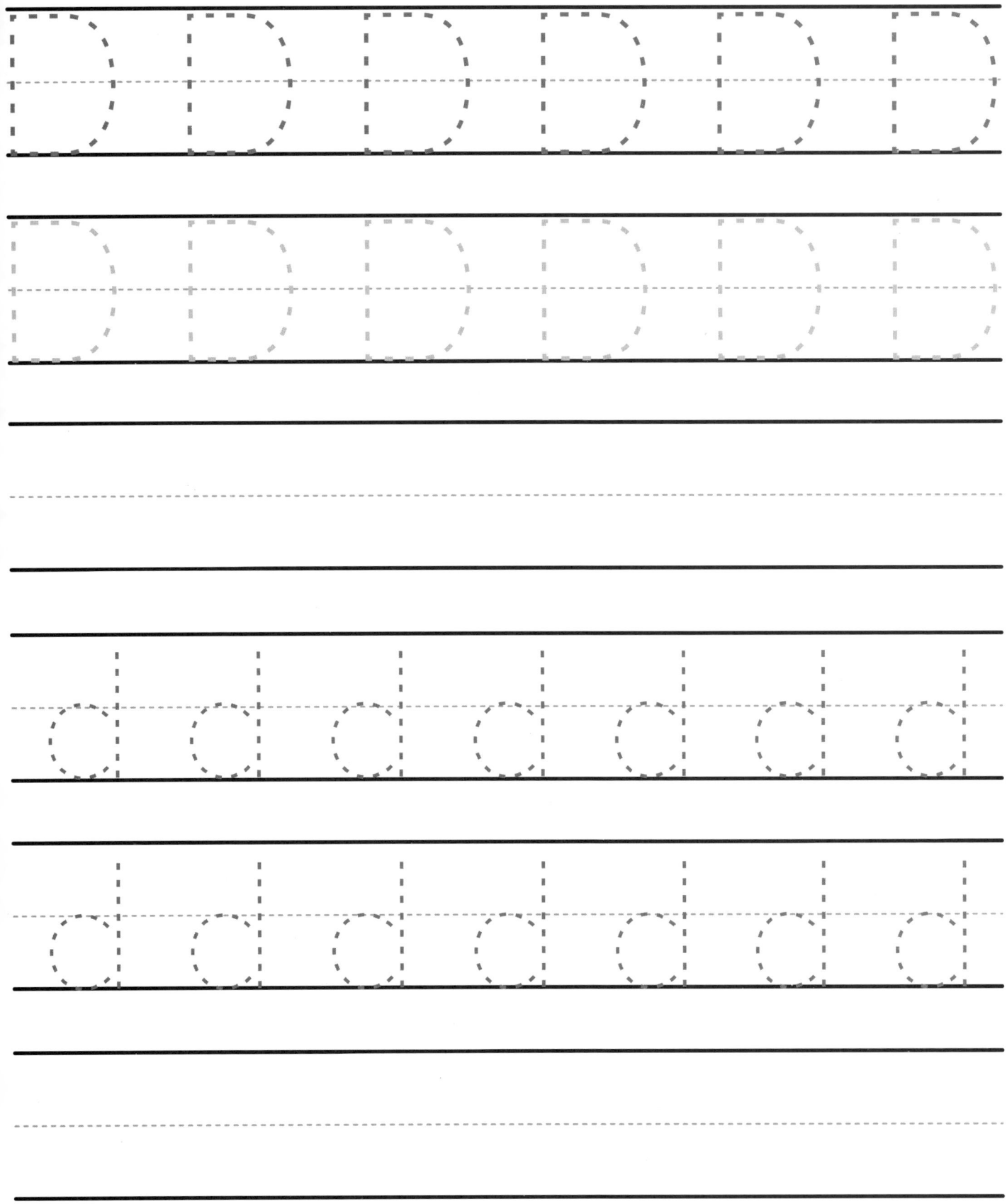

WRITE AND LEARN THE SIGHT WORDS.

do do do do

do

does does

does

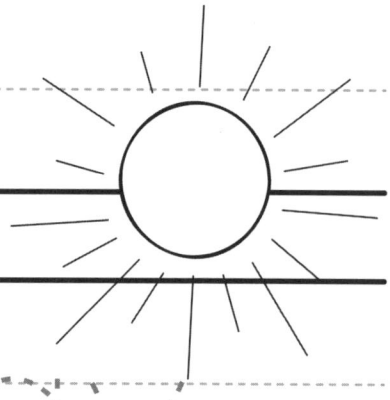

day day day

day

It's our best friend. Color it.

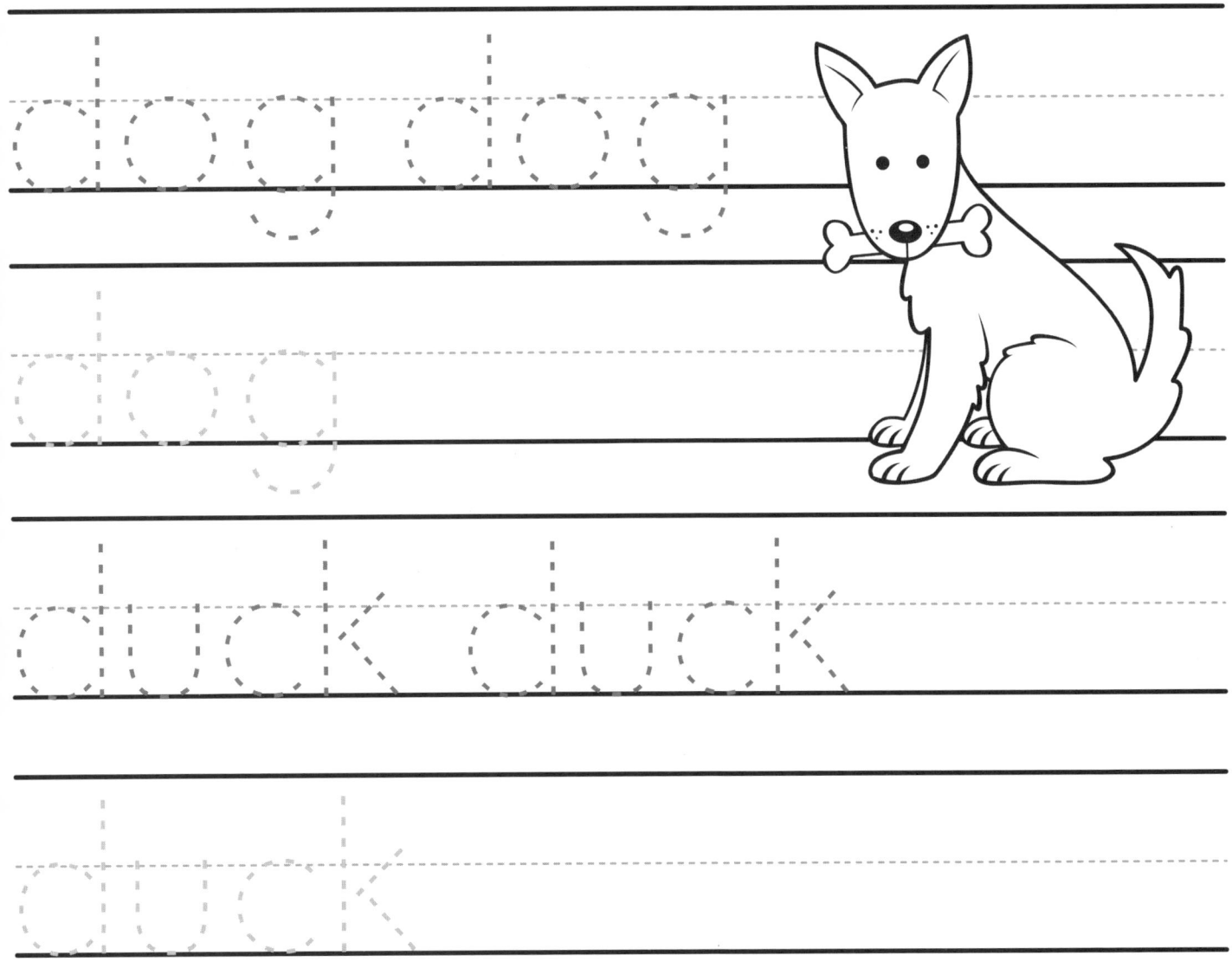

Which duck is different from the others?

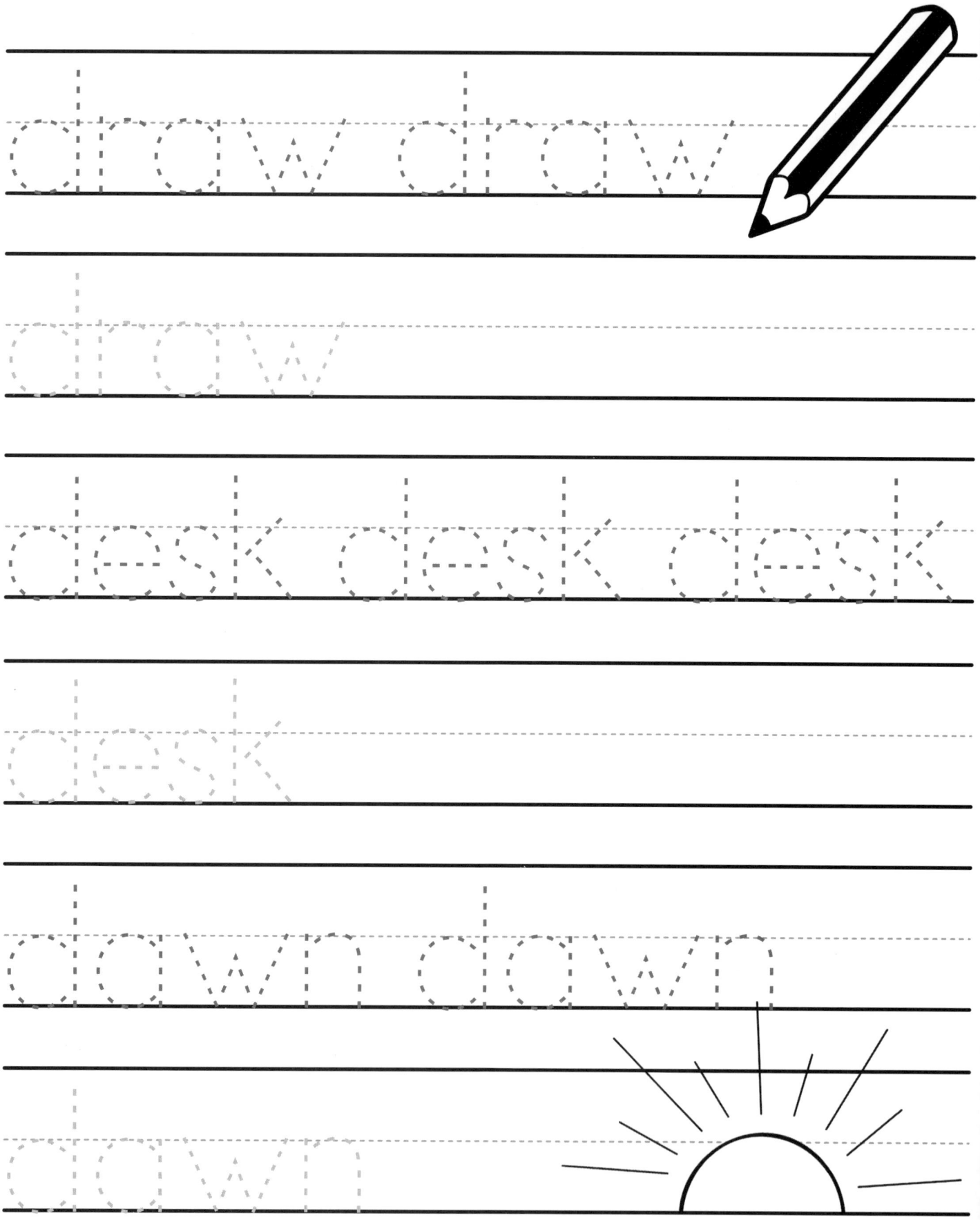
draw draw
draw
desk desk desk
desk
drawn drawn
drawn

d d

dance dance

d

dance

d d d

doctor doctor

d d

doctor

Which one does the doctor use?

★ **TRACE, WRITE, AND COLOR!**

Digby the dog

likes to play

in the park

all day

long.

★ **Color Digby the dog.**

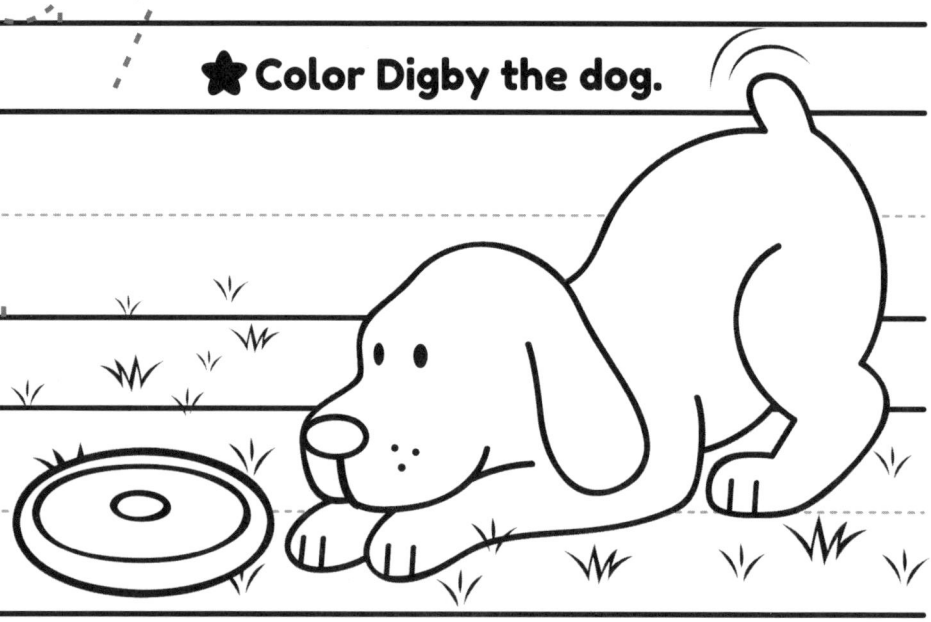

CAN YOU WRITE THE LETTERS BY YOURSELF?

WRITE AND LEARN THE SIGHT WORDS.

ear ear ear

ear

eat eat

Color the food that's good for you.

eat

and and and

and

egg egg egg

egg

★ **Trace and color the eggs.**

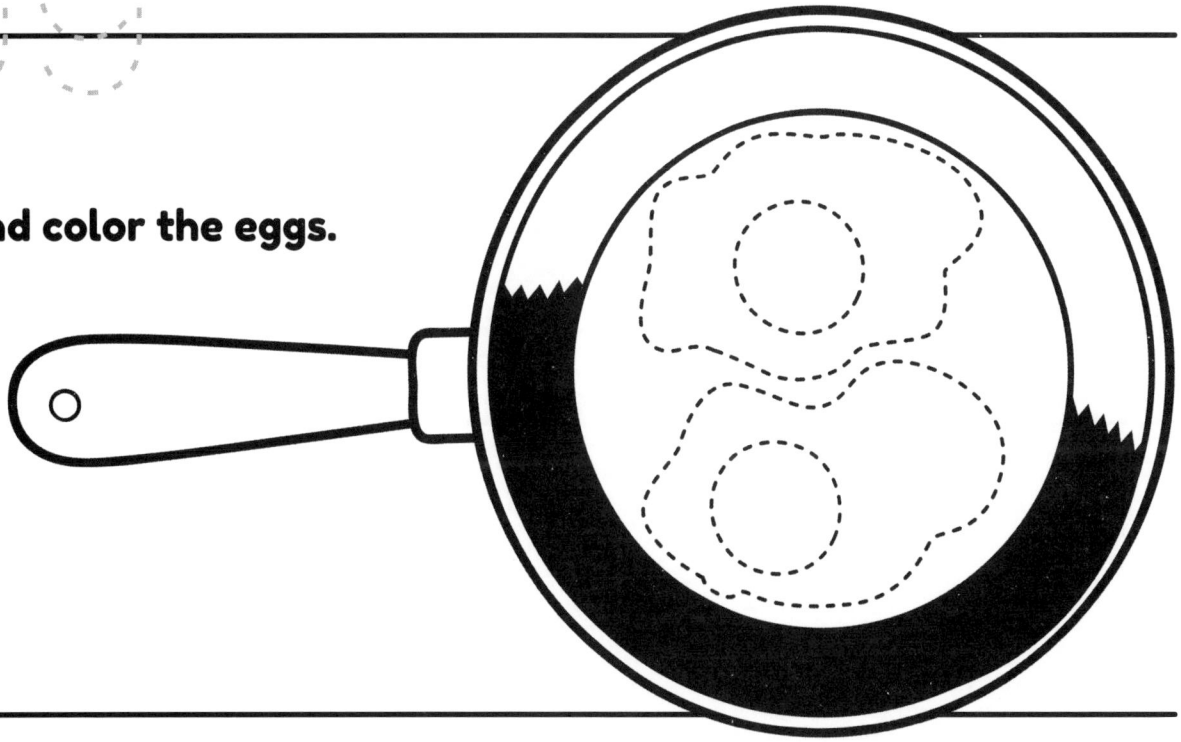

even even even

even

earth earth

earth

earth earth

earth

Do you know which one is the planet we live on? Color it.

early early

early

every every

every

elephant

elephant

TRACE, WRITE, AND COLOR!

CAN YOU WRITE THE LETTERS BY YOURSELF?

WRITE AND LEARN THE SIGHT WORDS.

for for for for

for

fly fly fly fly

fly

Color the bird.

few few few

few

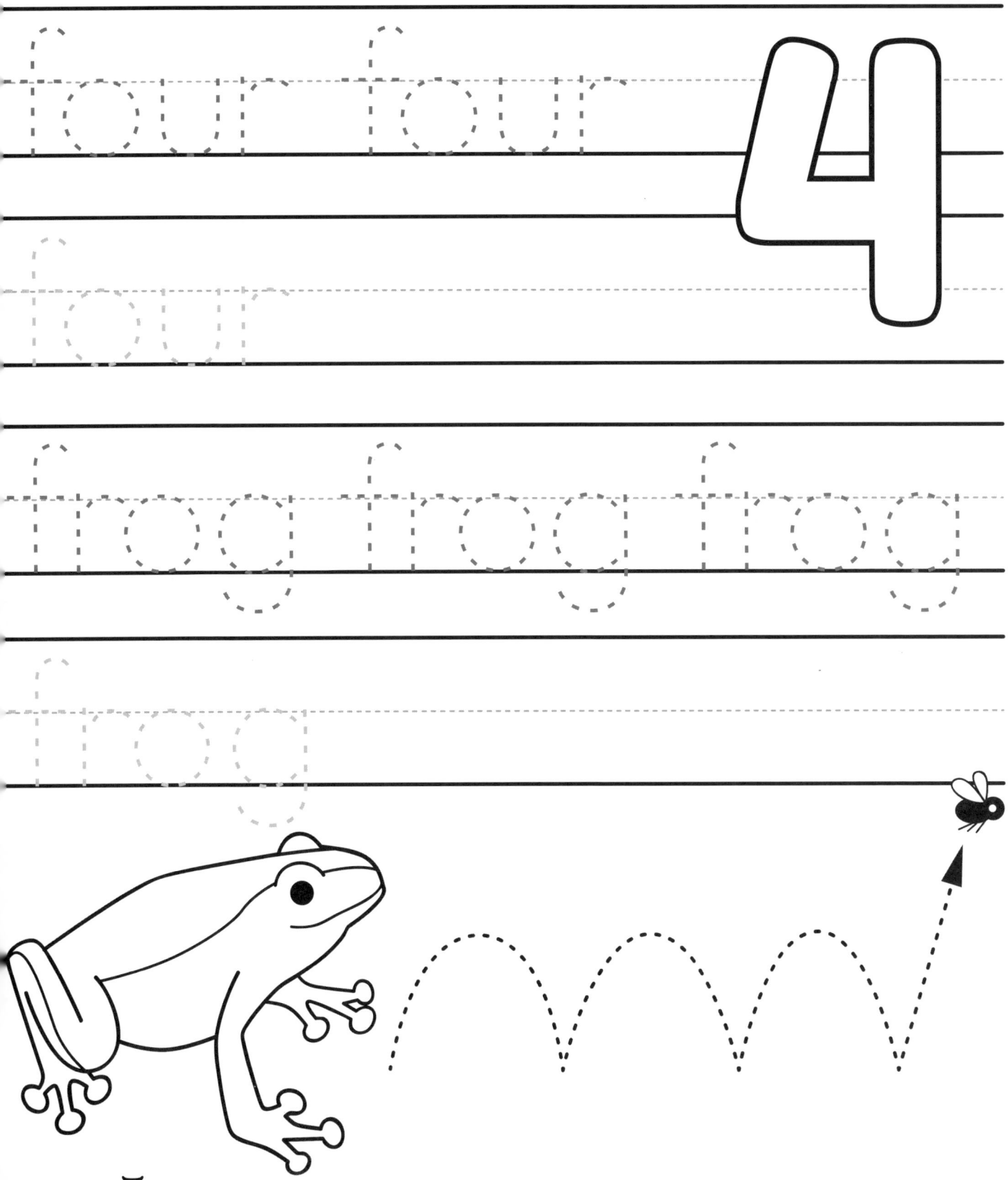

How many leaps does the frog need to catch the fly?

face face face

face

Draw a happy face, a sad face, and a mad face.

fork fork

What do we use a fork for?

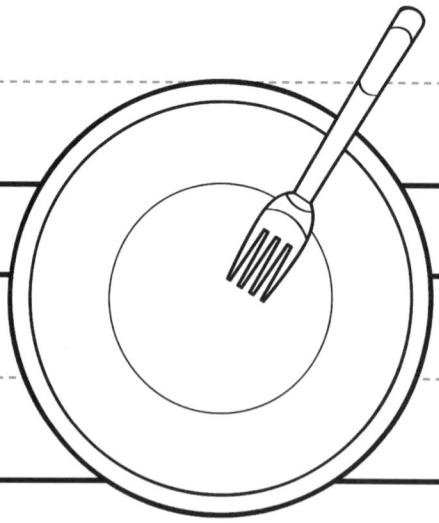

fork

fruit fruit fruit

fruit

★ **Color the fruit below.**

freedom

freedom

TRACE, WRITE, AND COLOR!

CAN YOU WRITE THE LETTERS BY YOURSELF?

WRITE AND LEARN THE SIGHT WORDS.

go go go go go go

go

get get get

get

good good good good good

good

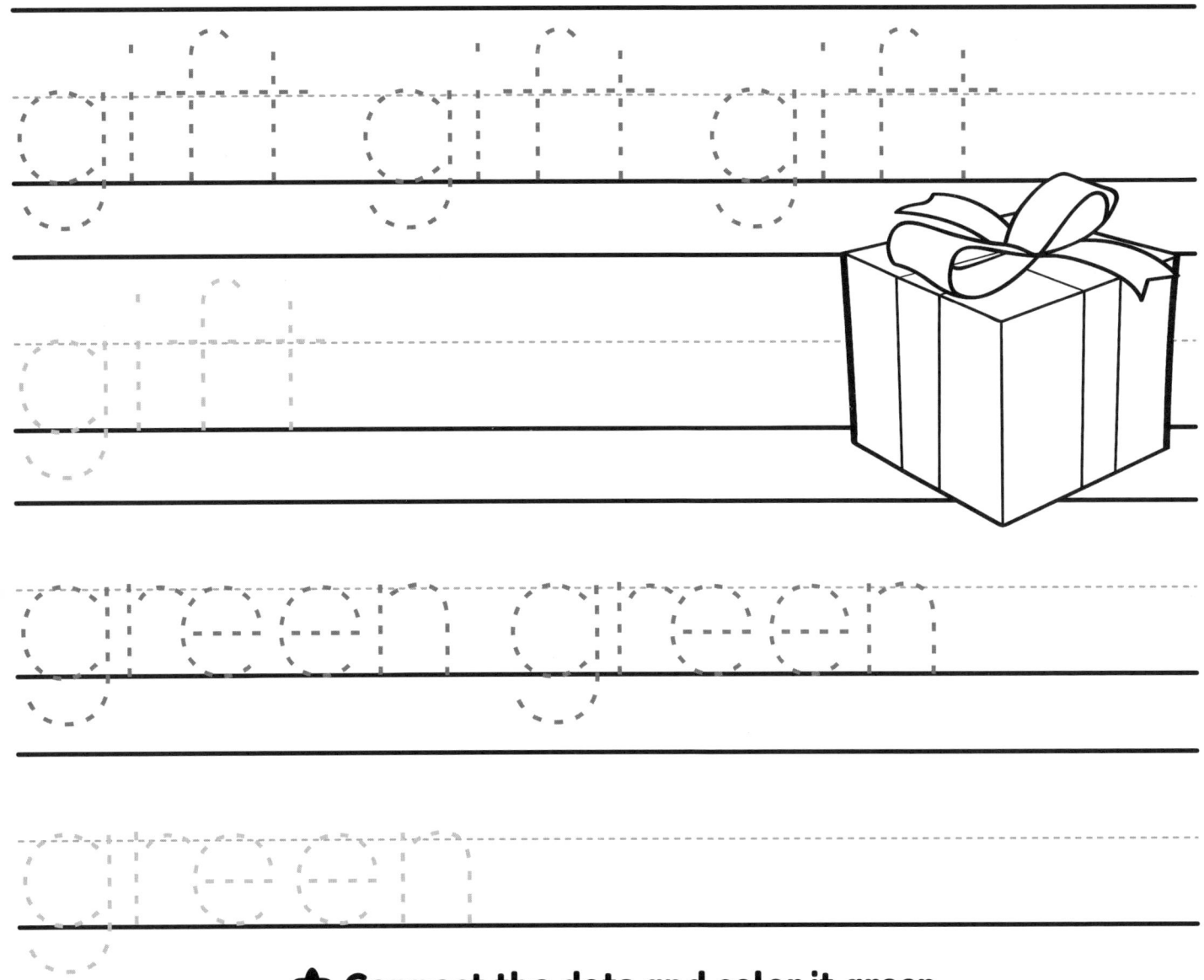

★ **Connect the dots and color it green.**

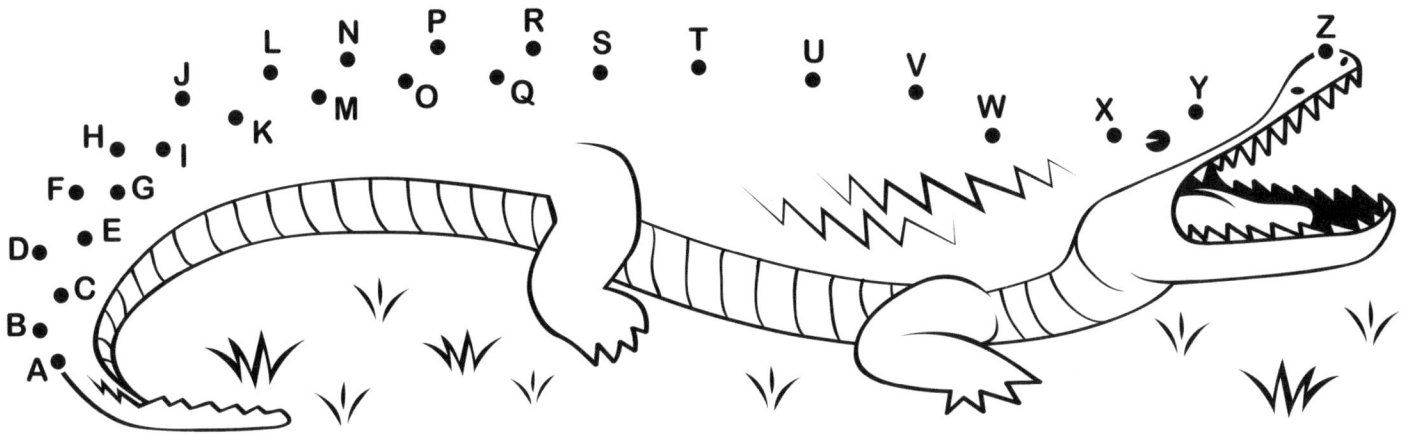

What game does this piece belong to?

game game

game

grow grow

grow

grape grape

grape

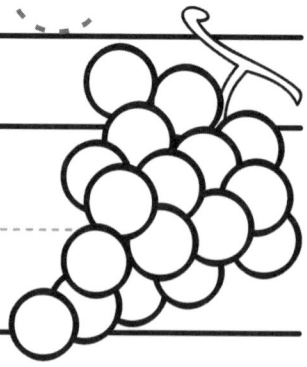

grass grass

grass

What is it called? Why?

grated grated

grated

grandmother

grandmother

TRACE, WRITE, AND COLOR!

Grandma has

a lovely green

cabbage patch

in her

garden.

CAN YOU WRITE THE LETTERS BY YOURSELF?

WRITE AND LEARN THE SIGHT WORDS.

the the the the the

the

then then

then

now now now

now

hot hot hot hot

hot

Color only the hot stuff.

have have have

have

hair hair hair

hair

★ **Give her different haircuts.**

home home

home

happy happy

happy

horse horse

horse

honey honey

honey

TRACE, WRITE, AND COLOR!

If I was a horse

I would run

and I would

prance

happily

all around.

CAN YOU WRITE THE LETTERS BY YOURSELF?

WRITE AND LEARN THE SIGHT WORDS.

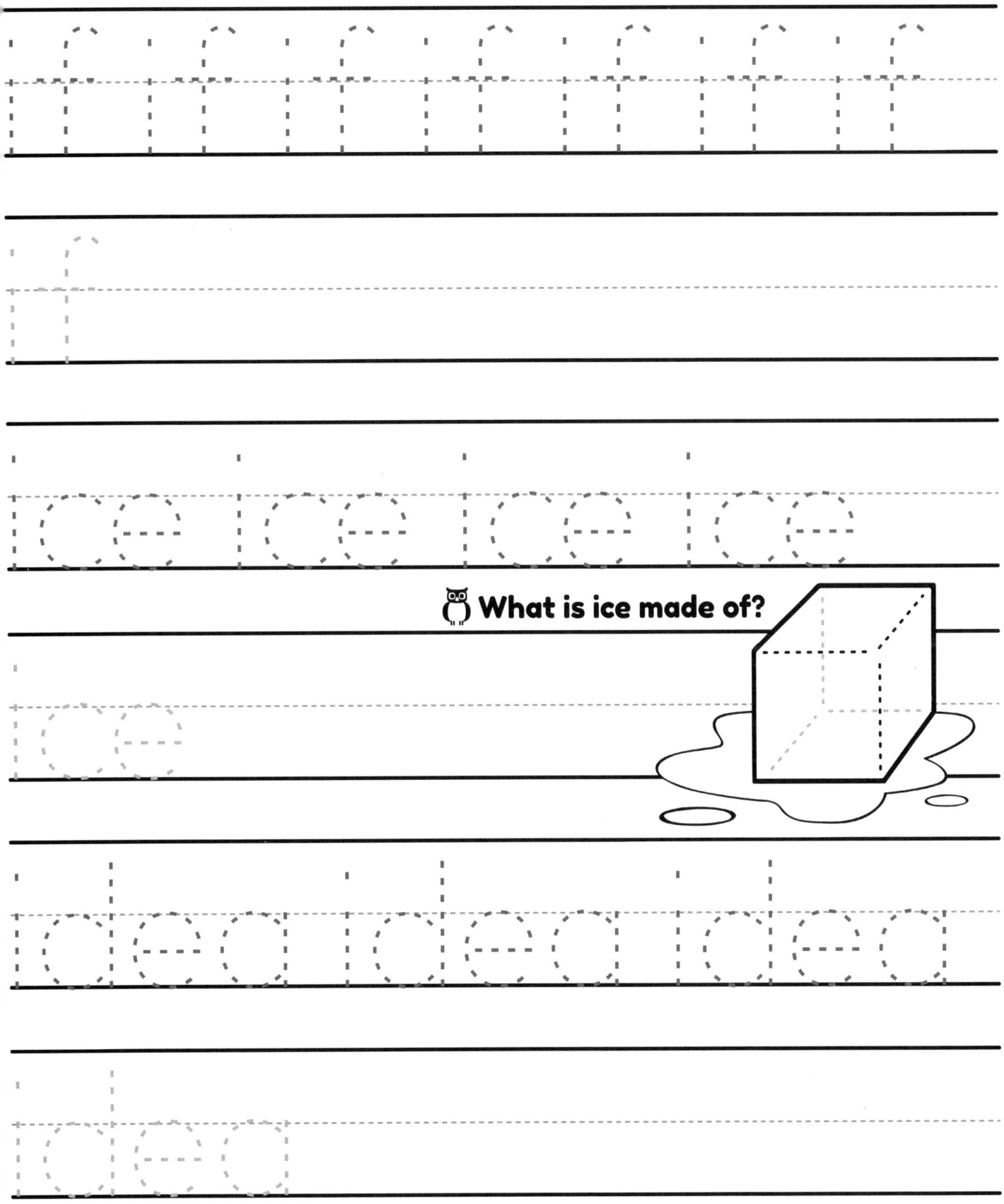
What is ice made of?

iron iron iron

What are horseshoes made of?

iron

invent invent

invent

Invent your own robots using the parts below.

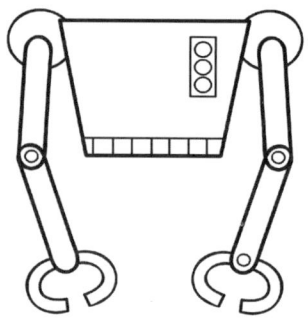

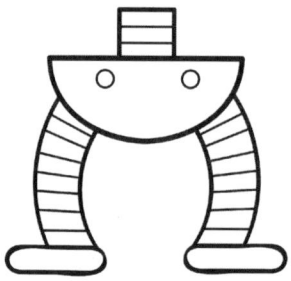

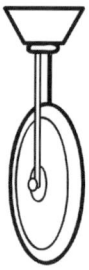

inside inside

Where does she live?

inside

island island

island

important important

important important

TRACE, WRITE, AND COLOR!

CAN YOU WRITE THE LETTERS BY YOURSELF?

WRITE AND LEARN THE SIGHT WORDS.

job job job job

job

joy joy joy joy

joy

Draw as much candy as you can inside.

jar jar jar

jar

join join join

join

Draw the missing paper doll to join them.

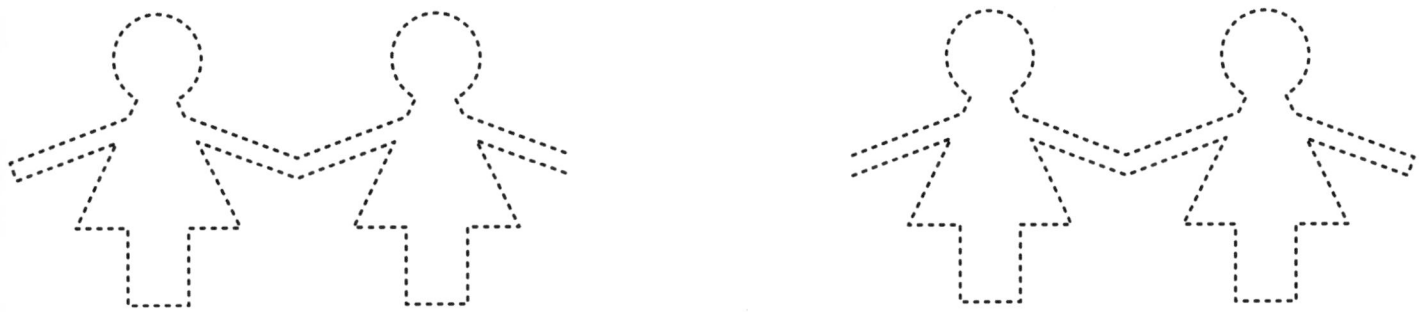

just just just

just

jump jump

jump

How many times does the rabbit jump to get the carrot?

juice juice

Color only the things you can make juice from.

juice

jelly jelly jelly

jelly

jungle jungle

jungle

Where does the monkey live?

jacket jacket

jacket

★ TRACE, WRITE, AND COLOR!

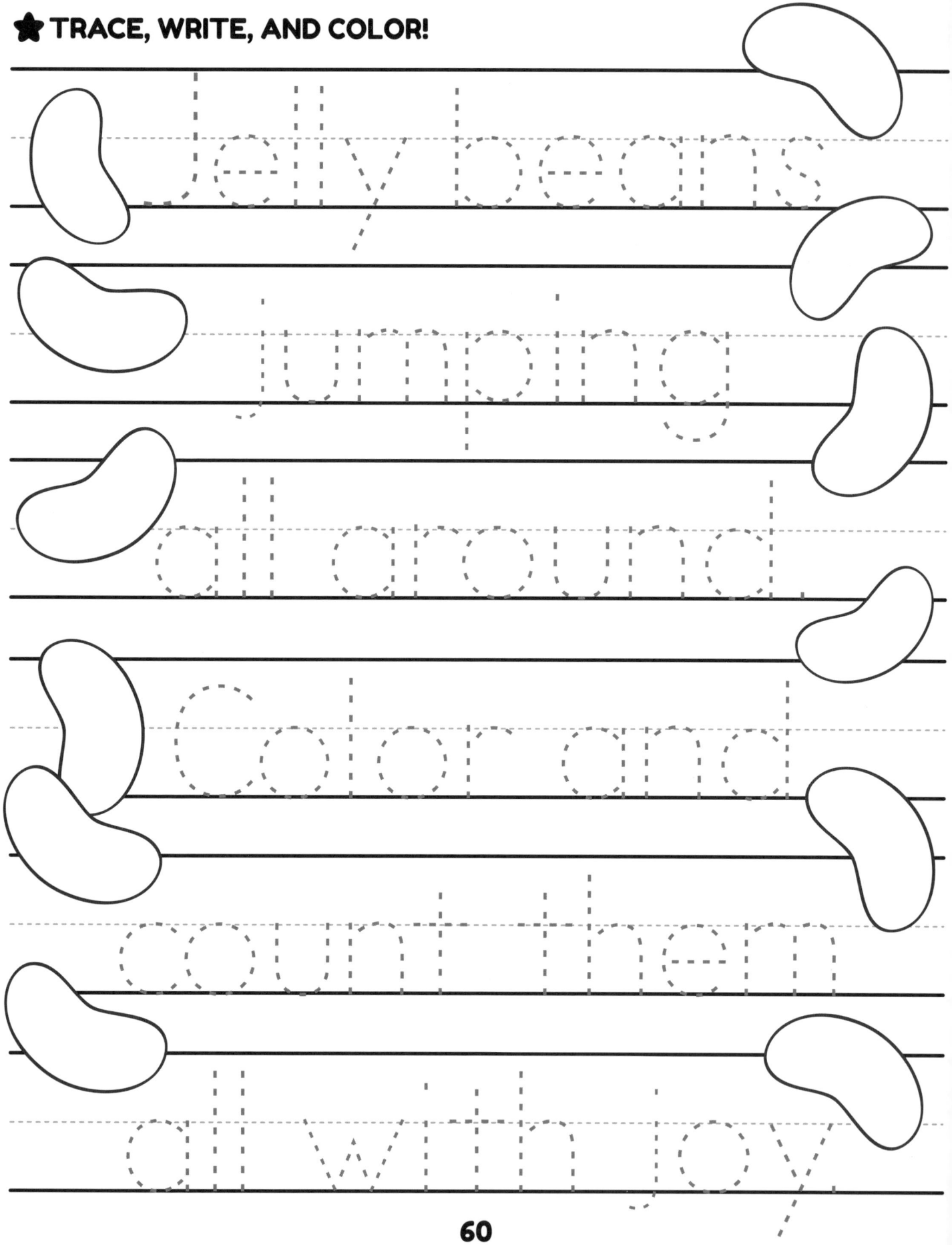

CAN YOU WRITE THE LETTERS BY YOURSELF?

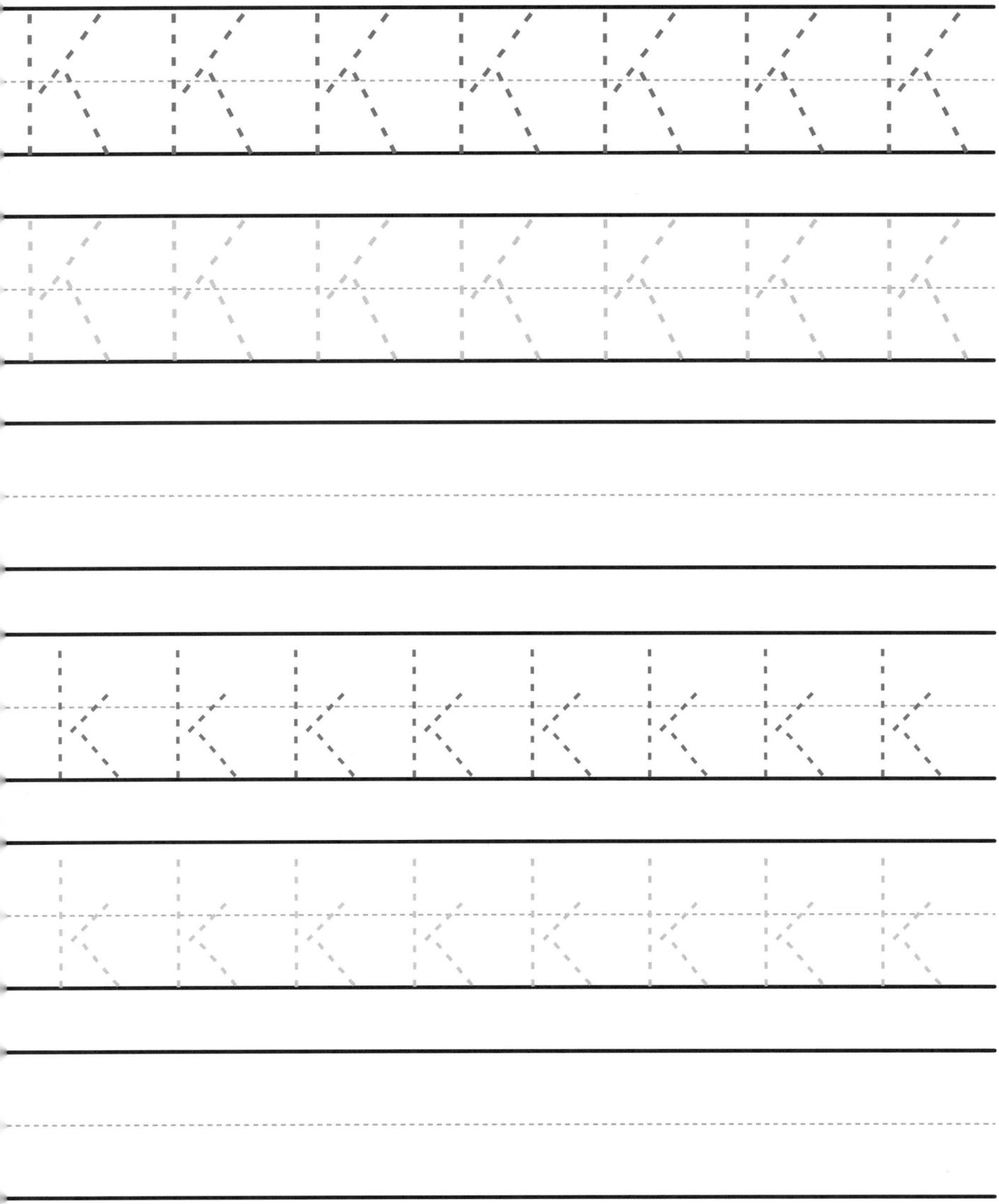

WRITE AND LEARN THE SIGHT WORDS.

key key key key

key

kiss kiss kiss

Give one to your Mom or Dad!

kiss

knee knee

knee

kite kite kite

kite

Decorate and color the kite any way you like.

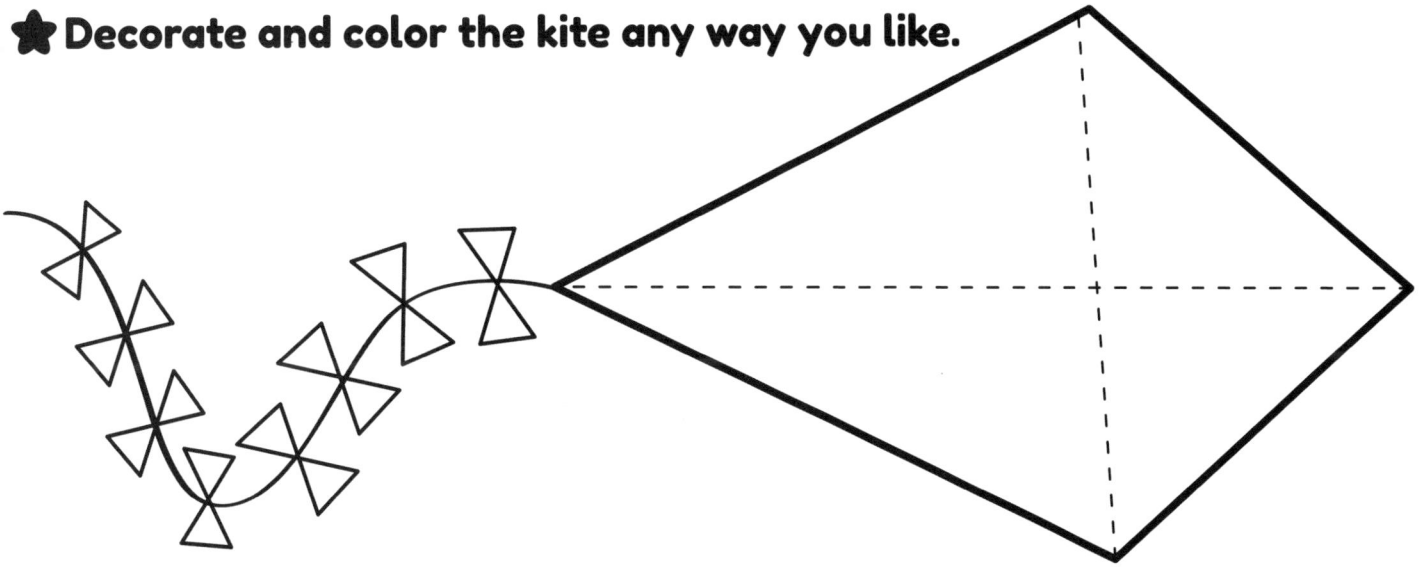

kick kick kick

What do we do with the ball?

keep

kind kind kind

kind

king king king

king

What would you do with the treasure?

keep keep

keep

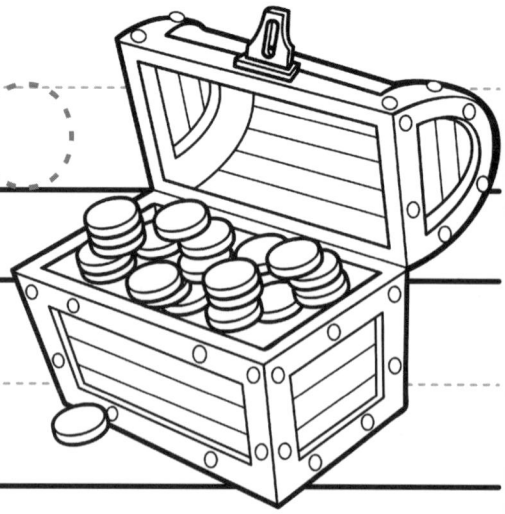

kettle kettle

What is a kettle for?

kettle

kitchen kitchen

kitchen

Where do we find all of these?

Can you draw another item below?

★ TRACE, WRITE, AND COLOR!

The kind king

lost his mane.

Give him one

he can

keep.

CAN YOU WRITE THE LETTERS BY YOURSELF?

WRITE AND LEARN THE SIGHT WORDS.

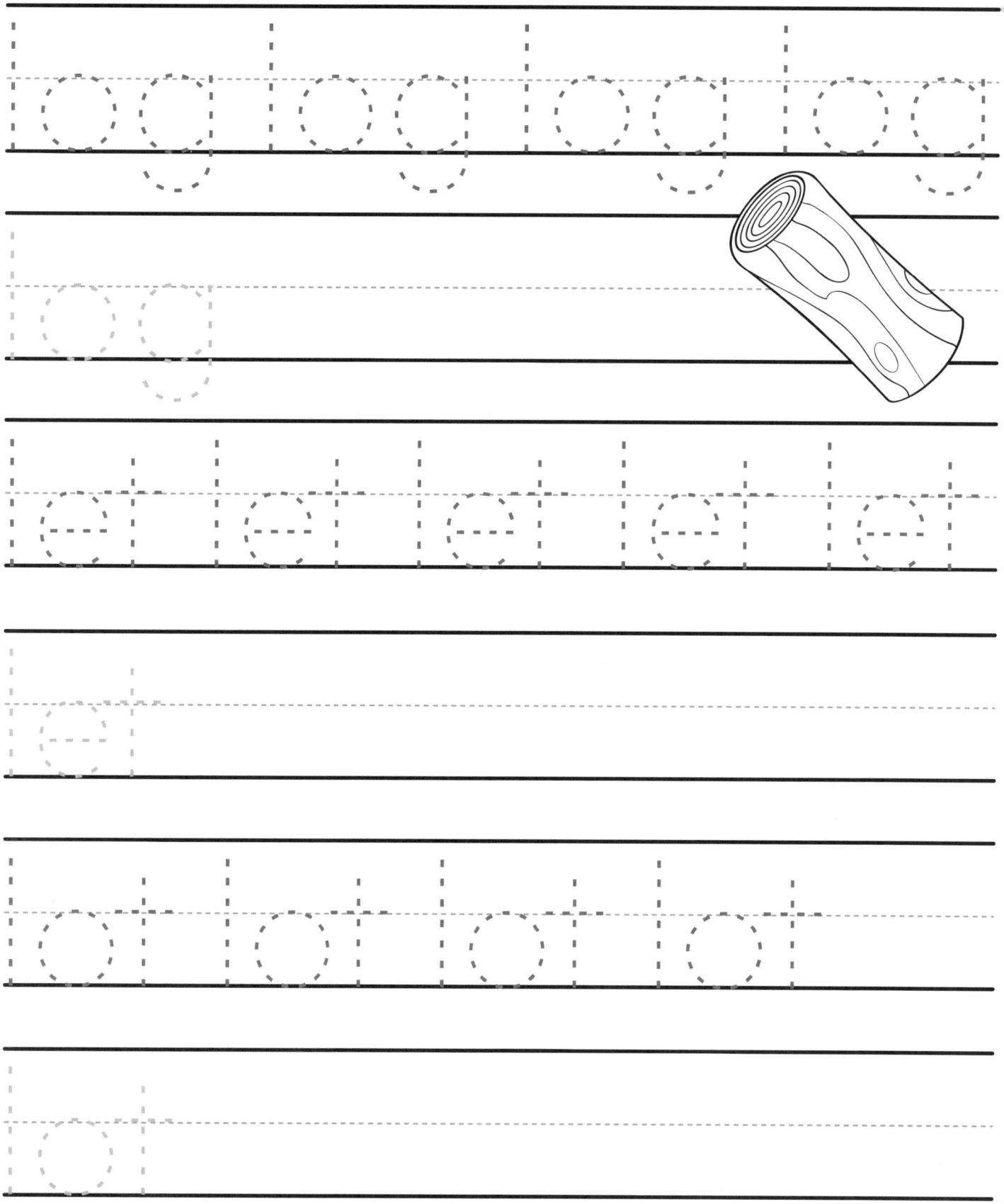

ess ess ess
ess
ove ove ove
ove
What does the heart stand for?
How many can you count?

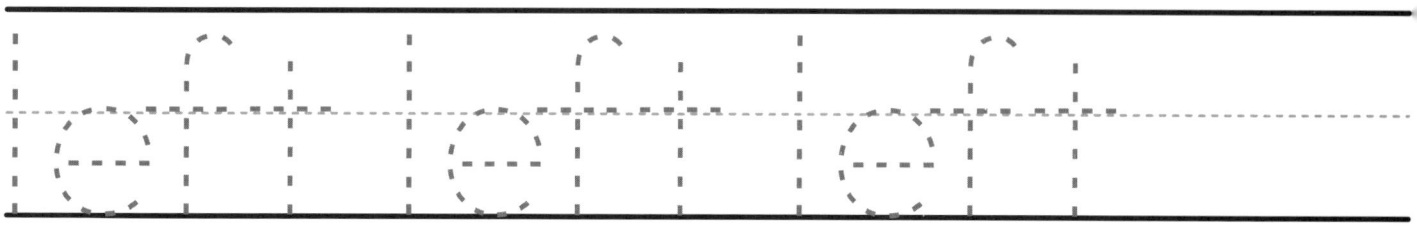

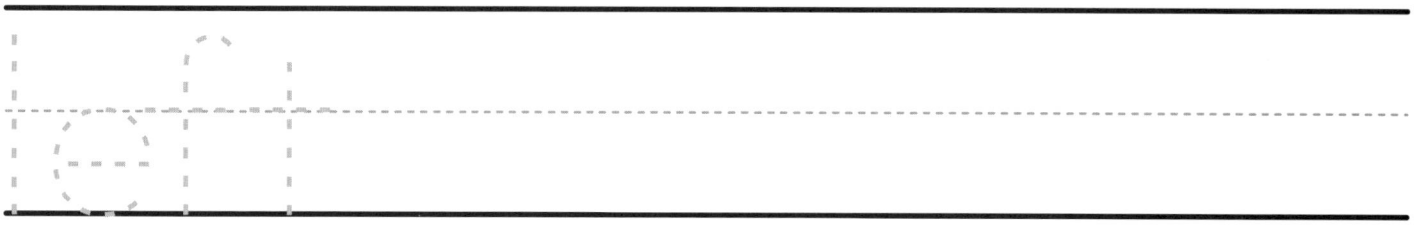

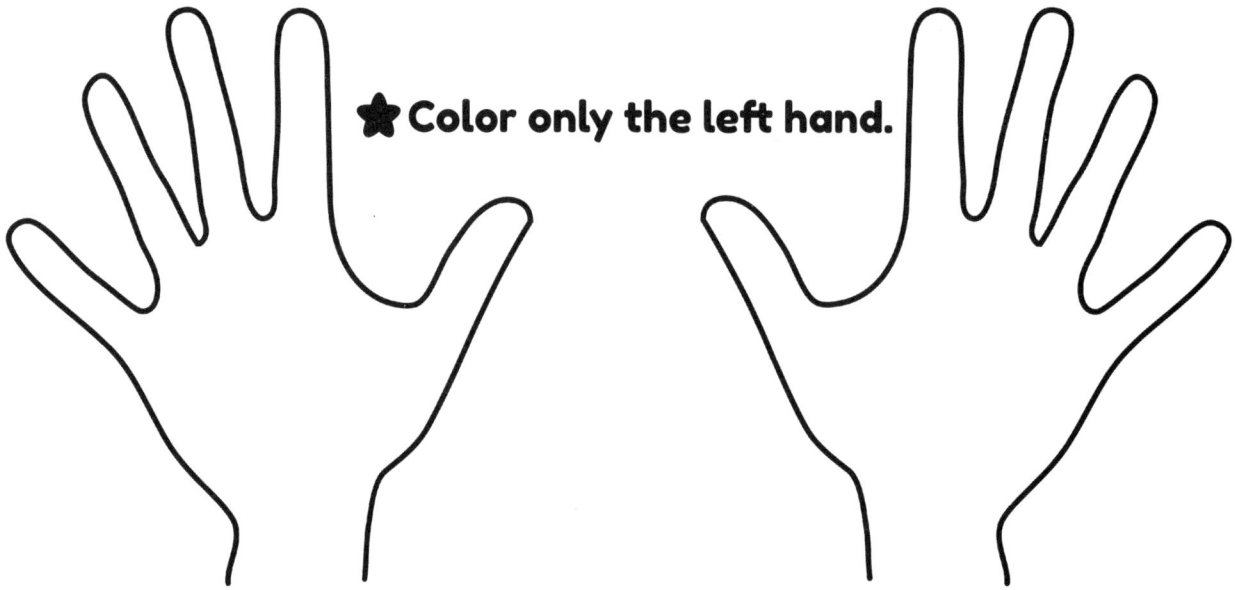

★ **Color only the left hand.**

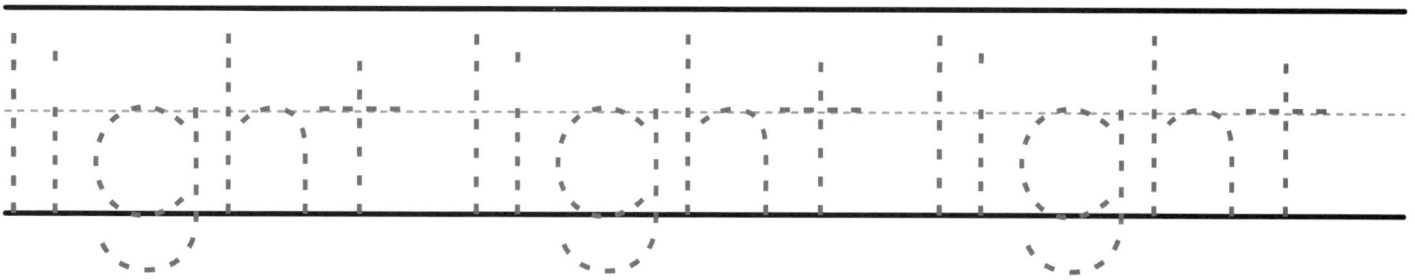

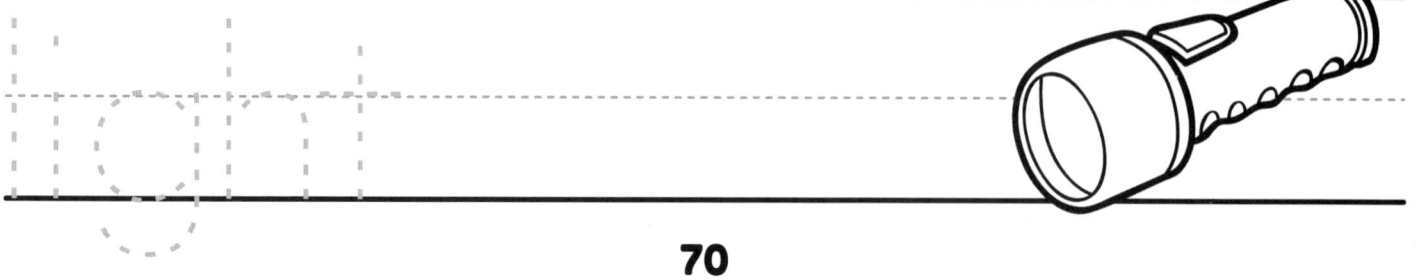

look look look

What are glasses for?

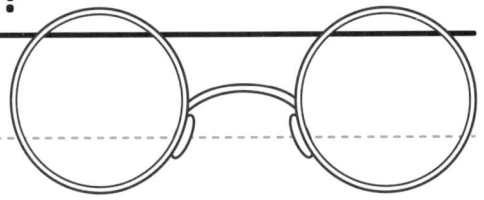

look

listen listen

Have you ever listened to this instrument?

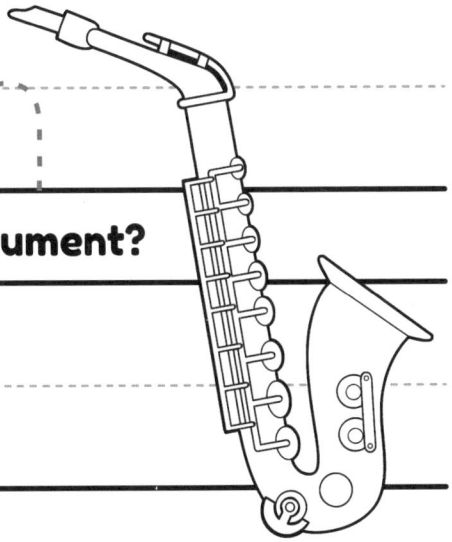

listen

learn learn

This is also an instrument. What is it for?

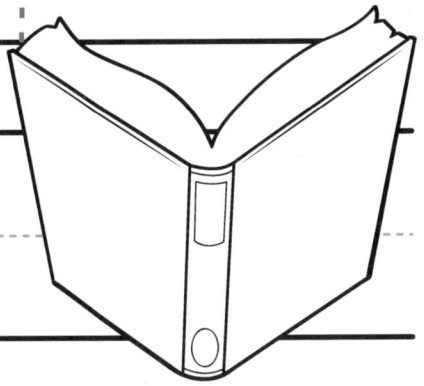

learn

★ TRACE, WRITE, AND COLOR!

CAN YOU WRITE THE LETTERS BY YOURSELF?

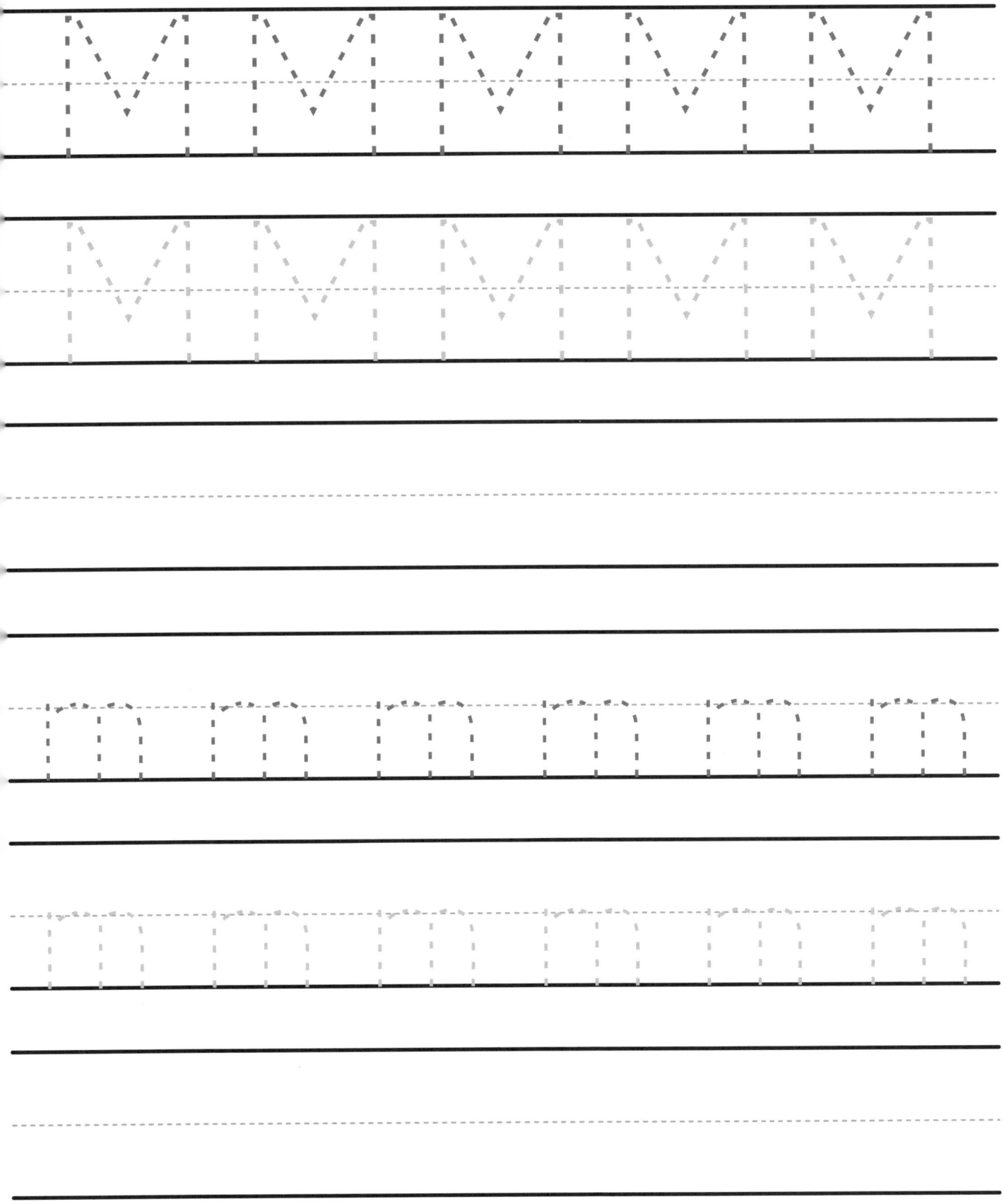

WRITE AND LEARN THE SIGHT WORDS.

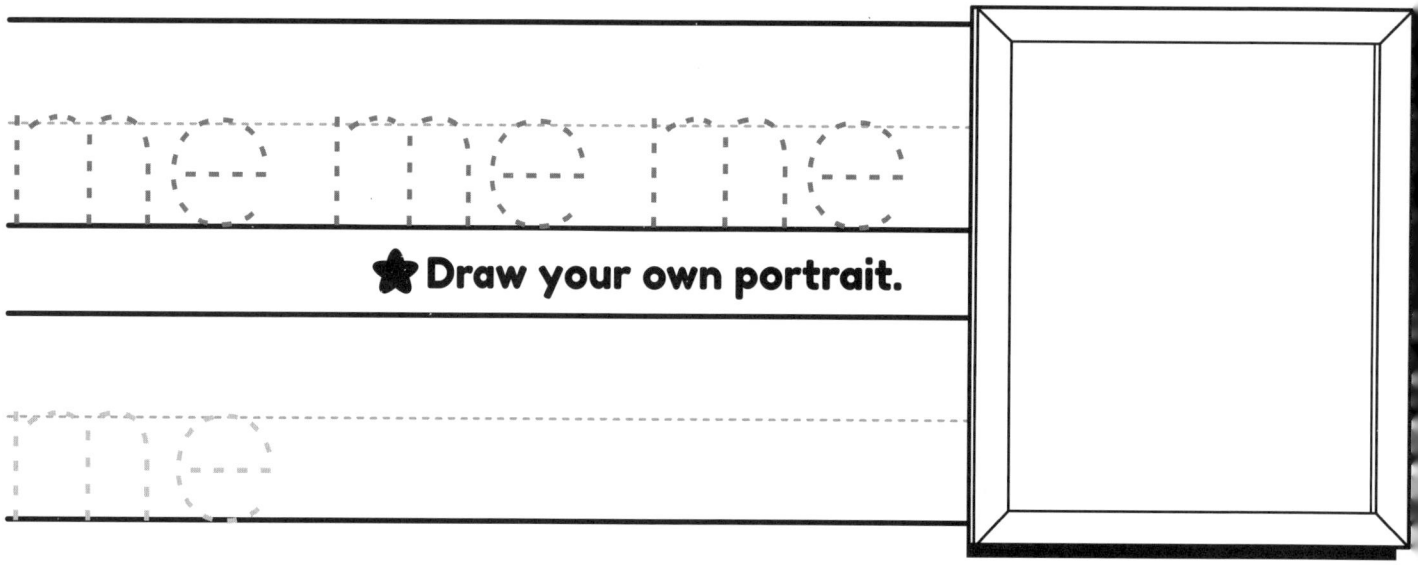

Draw your own portrait.

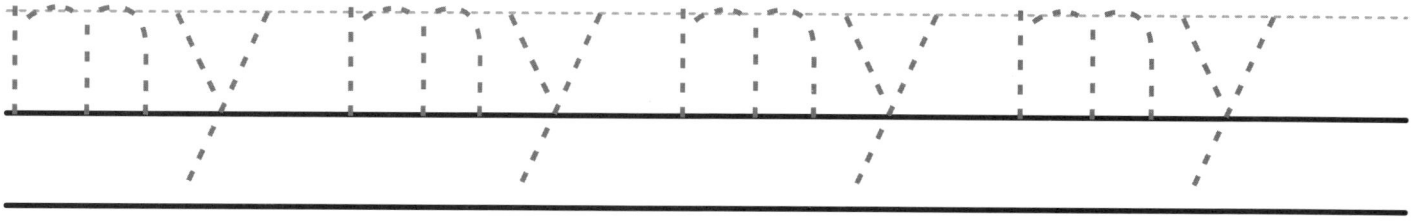

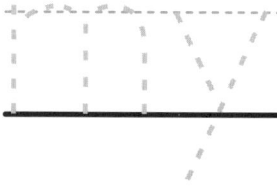

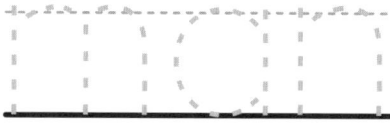

What country is this?
Fill each state with a different color.

maze maze

maze

Help the mouse out of the maze to find the cheese.

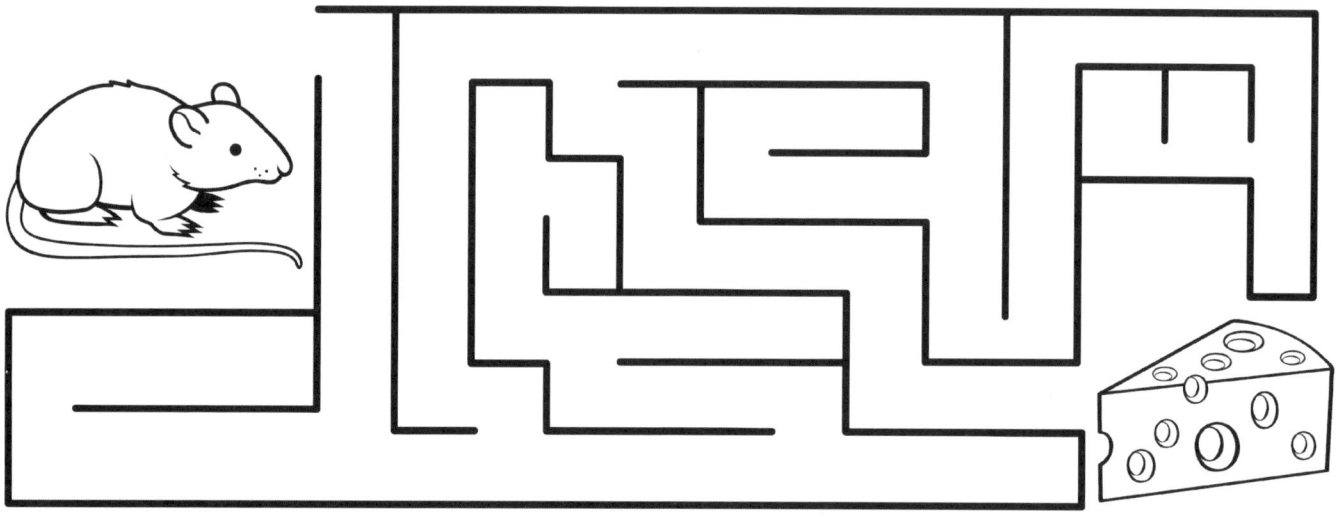

milk milk

Where does milk come from?

milk

meat meat

meat

What are most sandwiches made with?

mother

Draw your mom's portrait.

mother

TRACE, WRITE, AND COLOR!

My mother

likes to pour

milk into her

coffee

every

morning.

CAN YOU WRITE THE LETTERS BY YOURSELF?

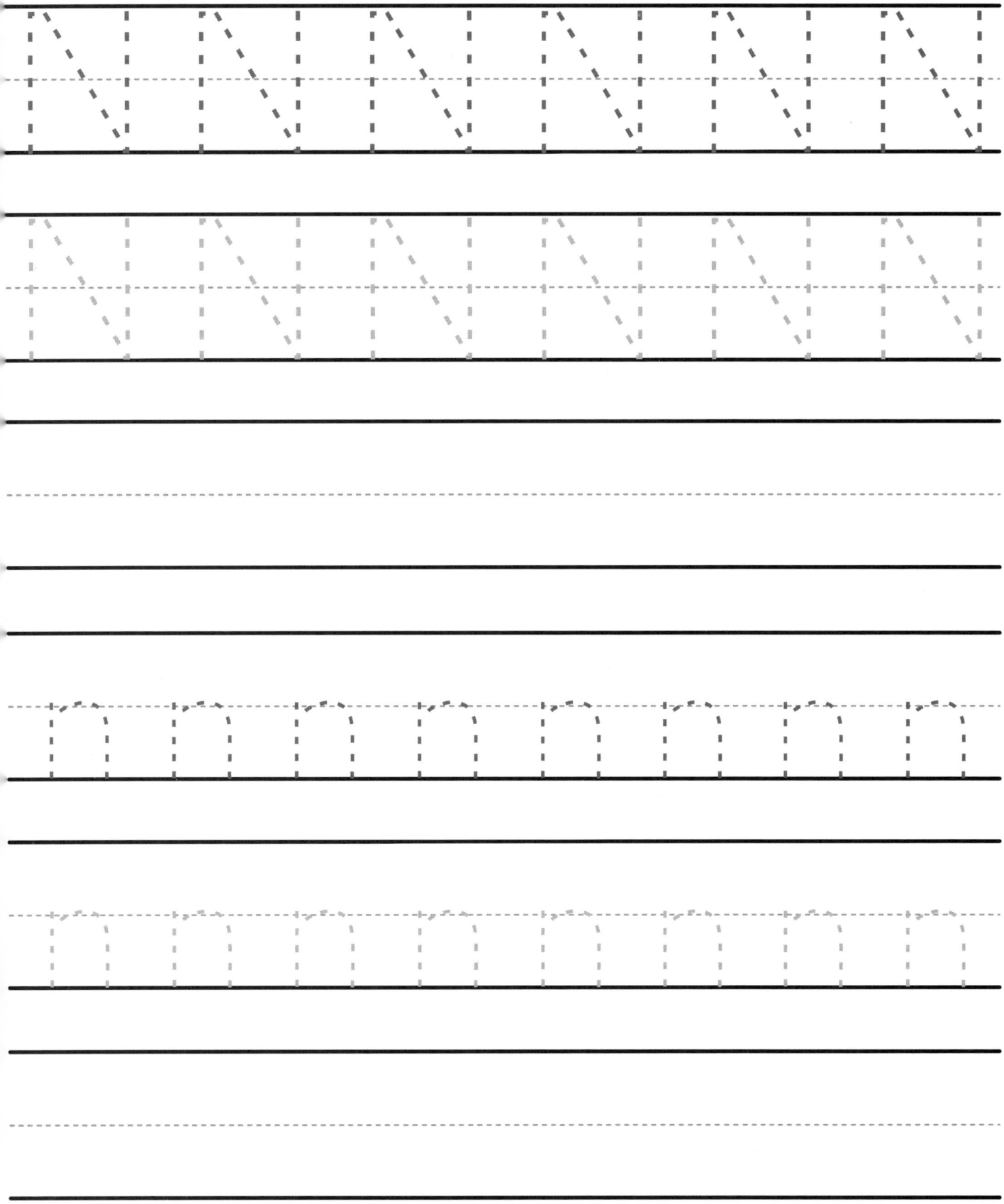

WRITE AND LEARN THE SIGHT WORDS.

NO NO NO NO NO

★ Color the sign red.

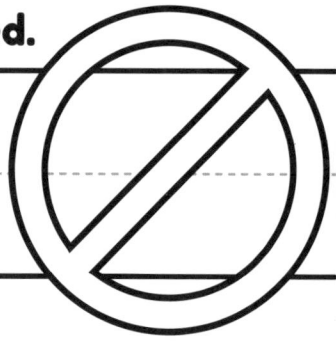

NO

NOW NOW NOW

NOW

NEW NEW NEW

★ Color this brand new toy car.

NEW

name name

name

★ **Can you write your first name below?**

★ **Can you write your last name below?**

nice nice nice

nice

nest nest nest

nest

★ **Trace the line, to help her reach her nest.**

near near near

near

need need

★ **If you need something, draw it here.**

need

nature nature

nature

number number

★ **Color the number that starts with N.**

1 2 3 4 5
6 7 8 9 10

number

★ TRACE, WRITE, AND COLOR!

Nadia the

nesting doll

always keeps

her nine gifts

near her.

A B C D E F G H I J K L M N **O** P Q R S T U V W X Y Z

CAN YOU WRITE THE LETTERS BY YOURSELF?

WRITE AND LEARN THE SIGHT WORDS.

of of of of of

of

THE UNITED STATES AMERICA

What is it missing?

of of of of of

of of of of of

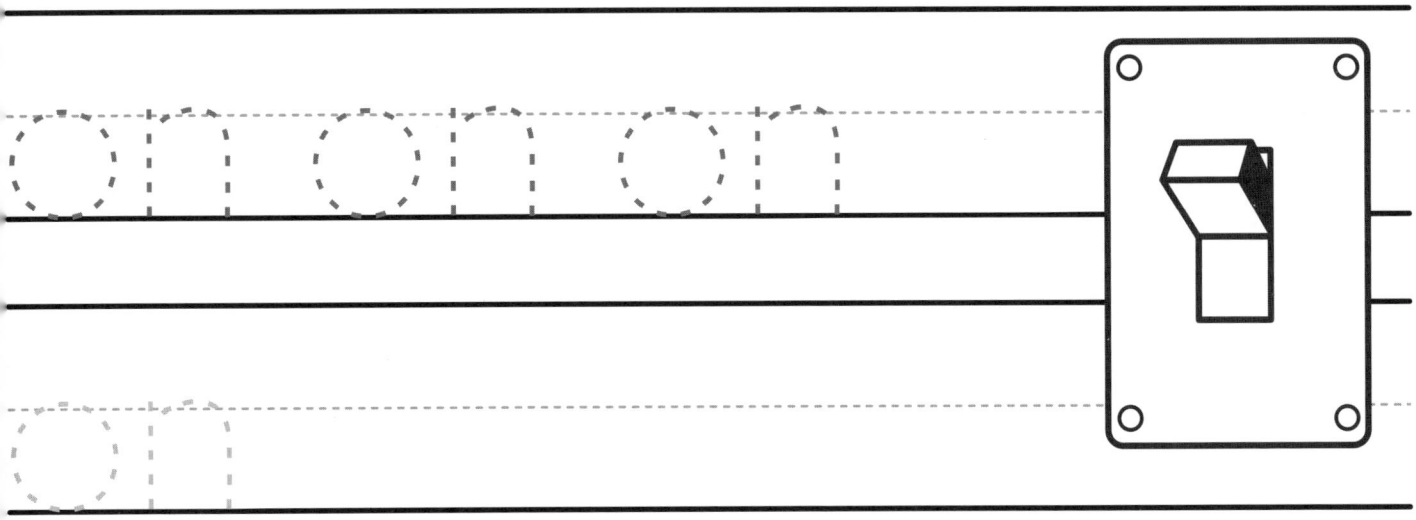

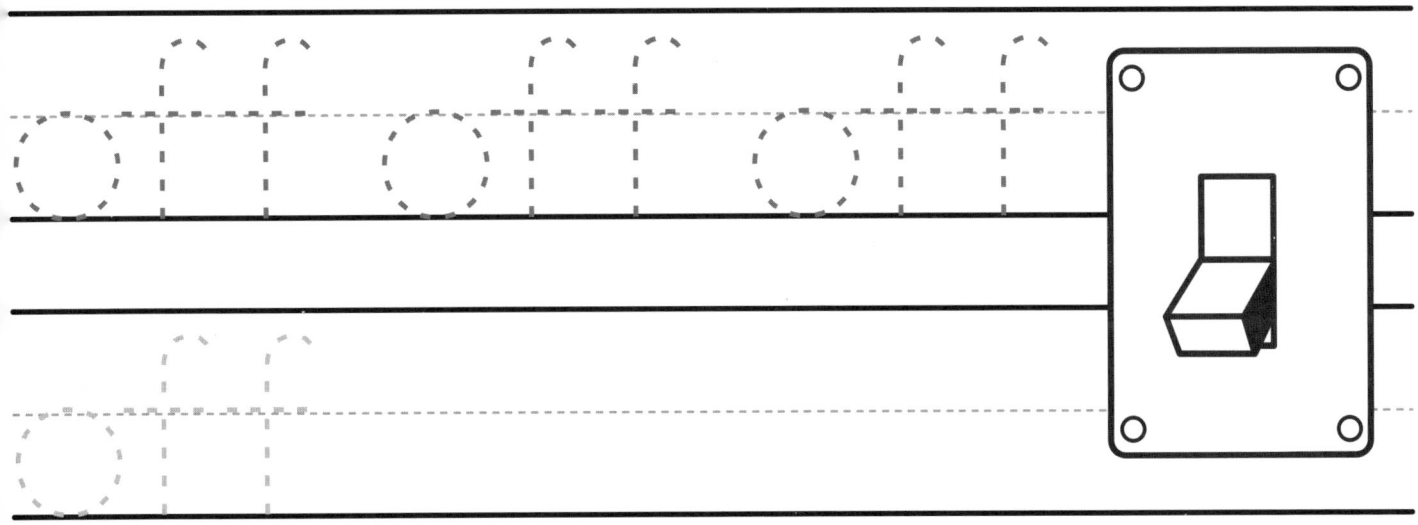

one one one

one

open open

open

owl owl owl

owl

How many owls are asleep?

once once

once

ocean ocean

ocean

They live in the ocean. What are they called?

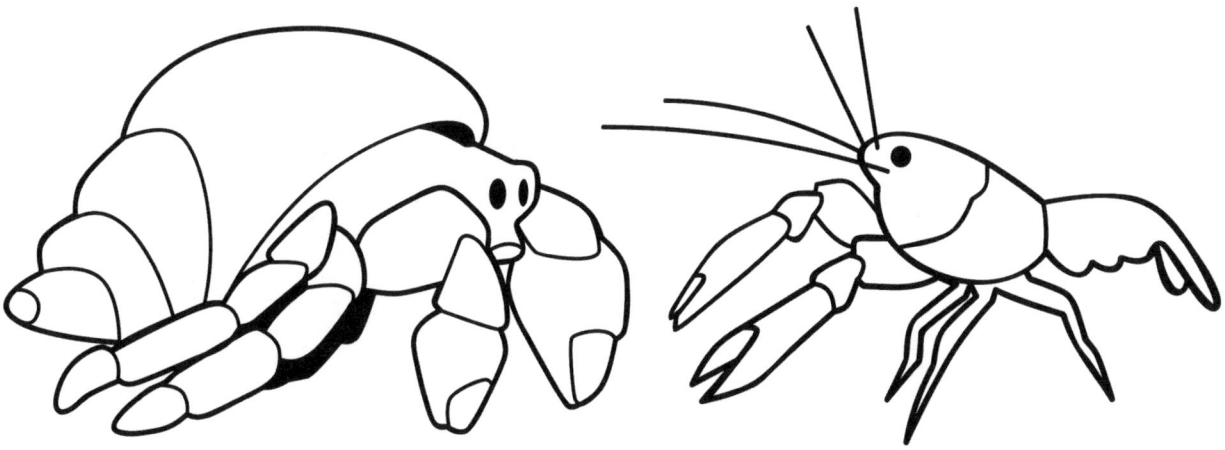

TRACE, WRITE, AND COLOR!

Once the

orca was seen

swimming in the

open ocean

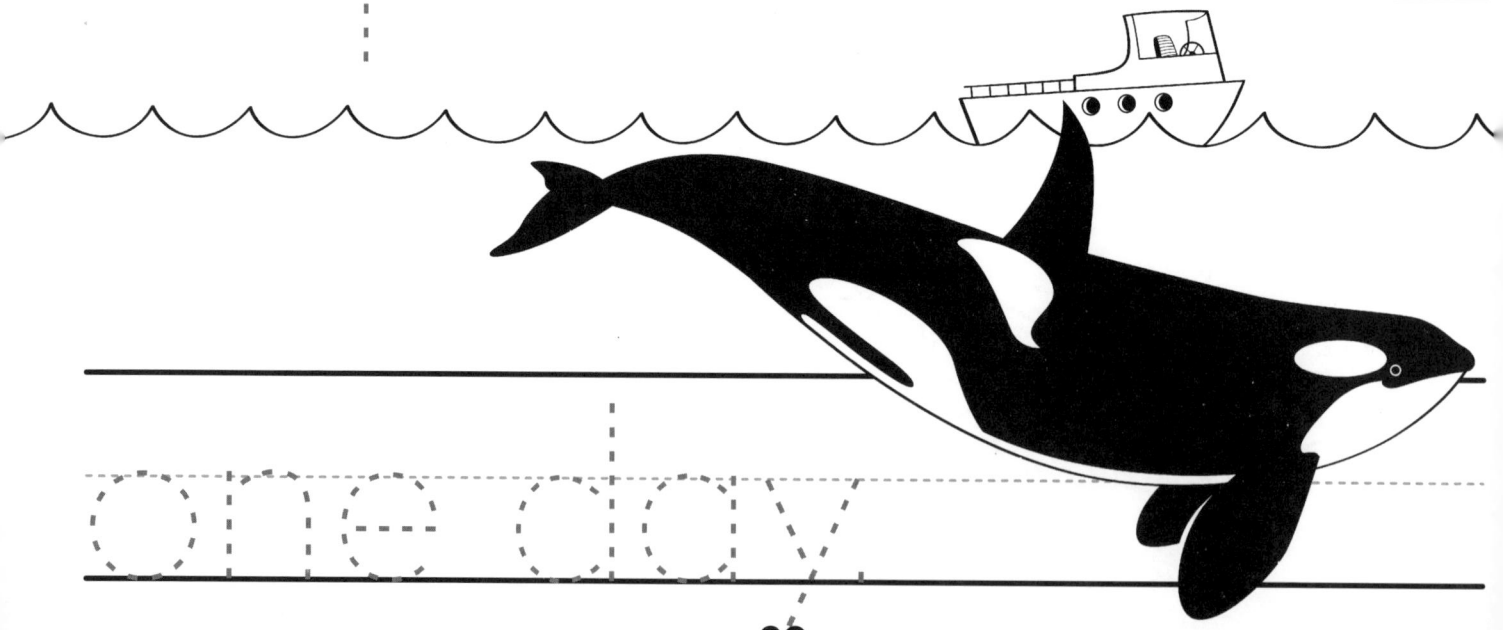

one day

CAN YOU WRITE THE LETTERS BY YOURSELF?

WRITE AND LEARN THE SIGHT WORDS.

pay pay pay

pay

What do we pay with?

Color the small coins red, and the big ones yellow.

pig pig pig

pig

pair pair pair

pair

★ **Color the cotton candy pink.**

pink pink

pink

Which sports do we play with each of the balls below?

play play play

play

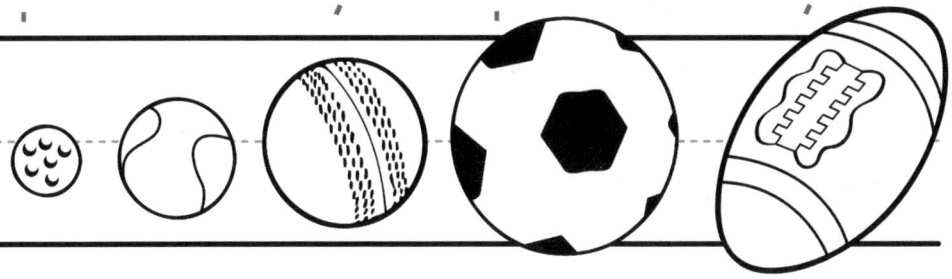

paint paint

What are brushes for?

paint

plane plane

plane

Which shadow doesn't match the plane?

pencil pencil

pencil

people people

people

Where does this fruit come from?

pineapple

pineapple

TRACE, WRITE, AND COLOR!

The pink pig
points himself
down with
mud from his
pigpen.

CAN YOU WRITE THE LETTERS BY YOURSELF?

WRITE AND LEARN THE SIGHT WORDS.

quiz quiz

quiz

quite quite

quite

quest quest

quest

quilt quilt

quilt

quiet quiet

quiet

quick quick

quick

quack quack

quack

What noise does each animal make? Which one quacks?

queen queen

queen

quarter

quarter

What is the difference between a question and a quiz?

question

question

question

Write the word on your own.

TRACE, WRITE, AND COLOR!

Quiet little

rabbits

are known

for being

quite quick

on their feet.

CAN YOU WRITE THE LETTERS BY YOURSELF?

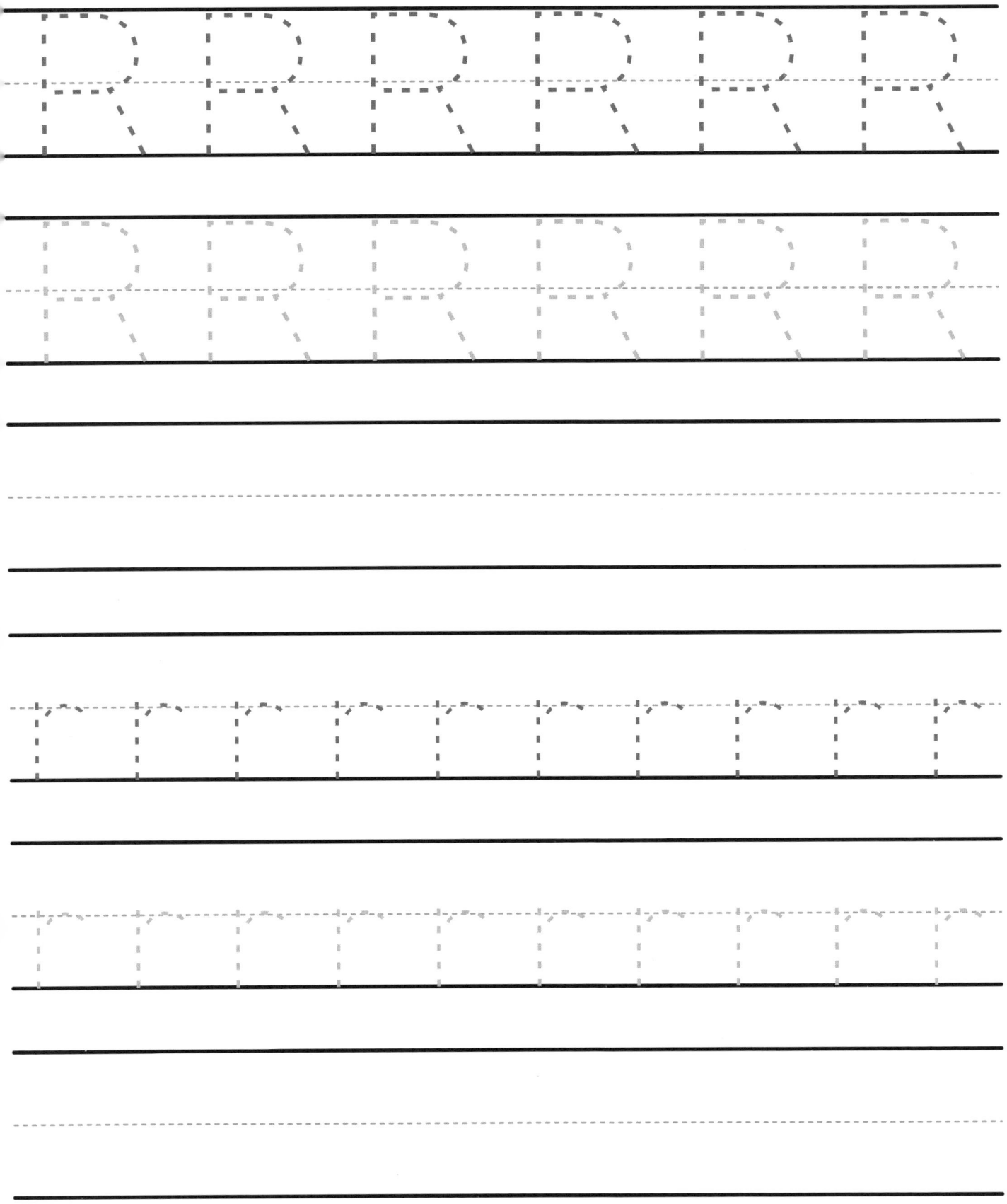

WRITE AND LEARN THE SIGHT WORDS.

red red red red

★ Color them red.

red

run run run run run

run

rat rat rat rat rat

Where do rats live?

rat

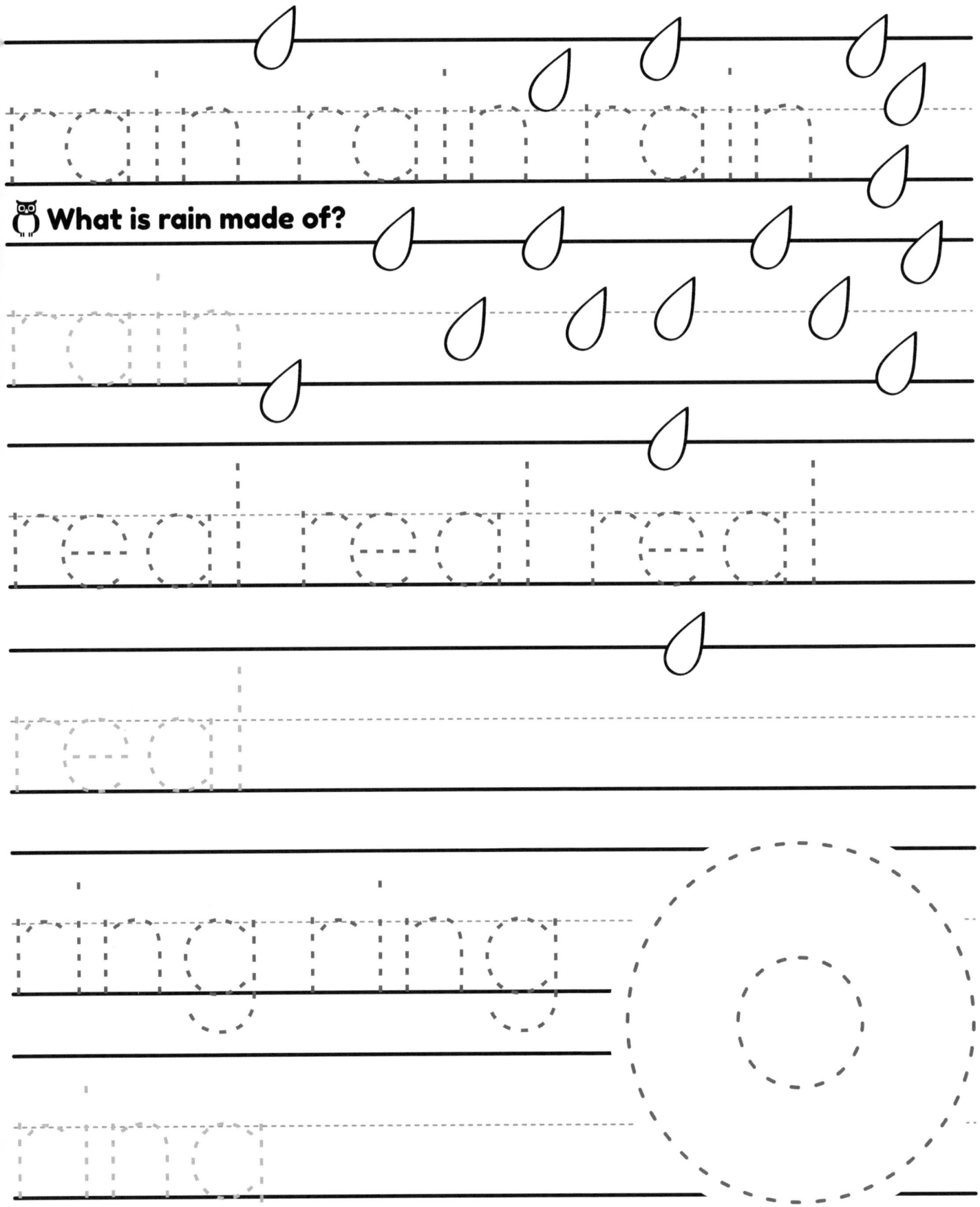

What is rain made of?

radio radio

radio

right right

right

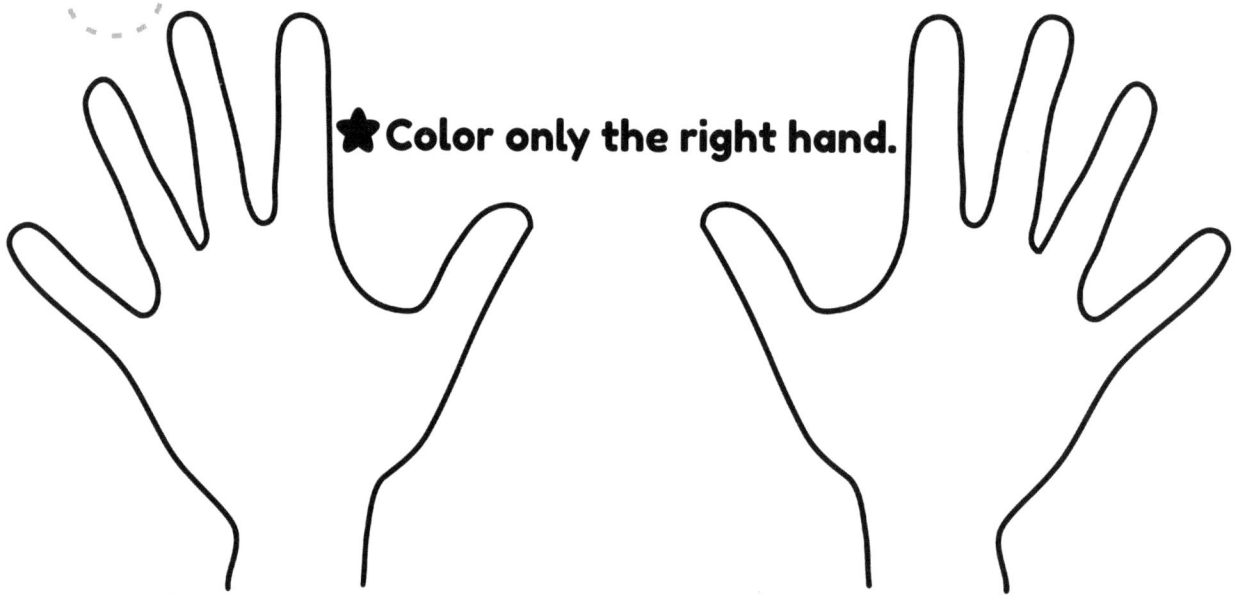

★ **Color only the right hand.**

repair repair

repair

restaurant

restaurant

The table is set. Do you know the name of each item?

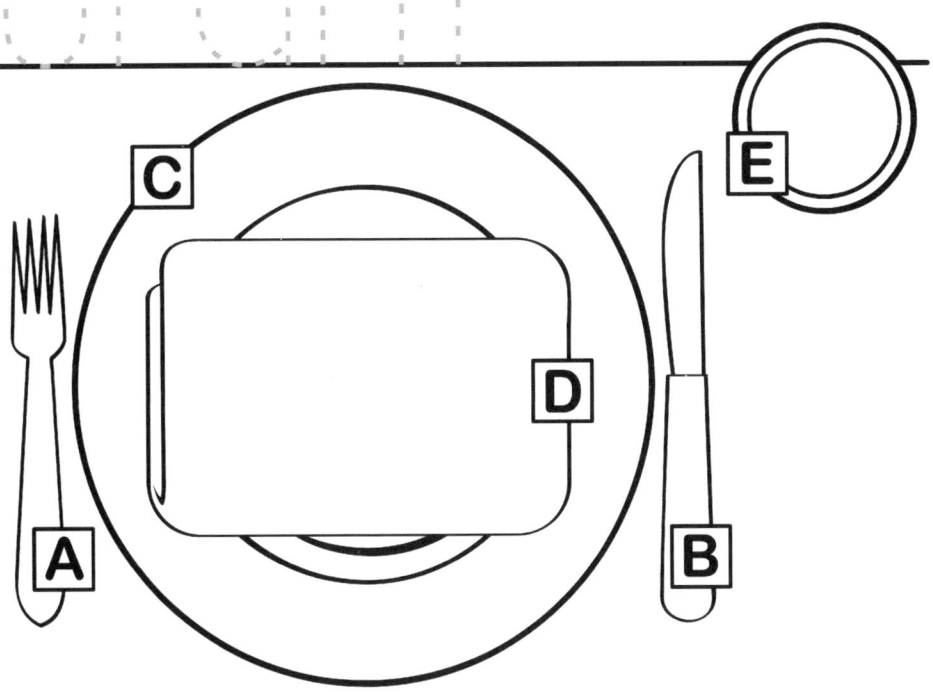

TRACE, WRITE, AND COLOR!

Ringo the rat

loves to listen

to rock music

on the

radio.

CAN YOU WRITE THE LETTERS BY YOURSELF?

WRITE AND LEARN THE SIGHT WORDS.

SO SO SO SO SO

SO

SUN SUN SUN SUN

Color it.

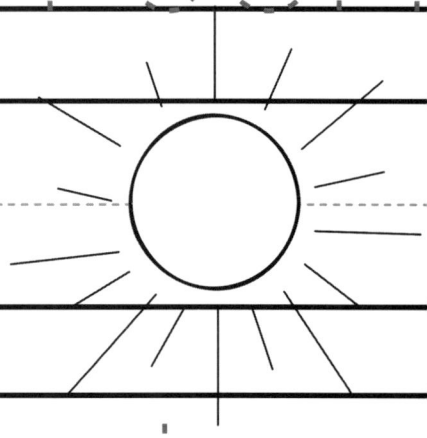

SUN

SOAP SOAP SOAP

SOAP

say say say

say

see see

What do you like seeing on TV?

see

sea sea sea

sea

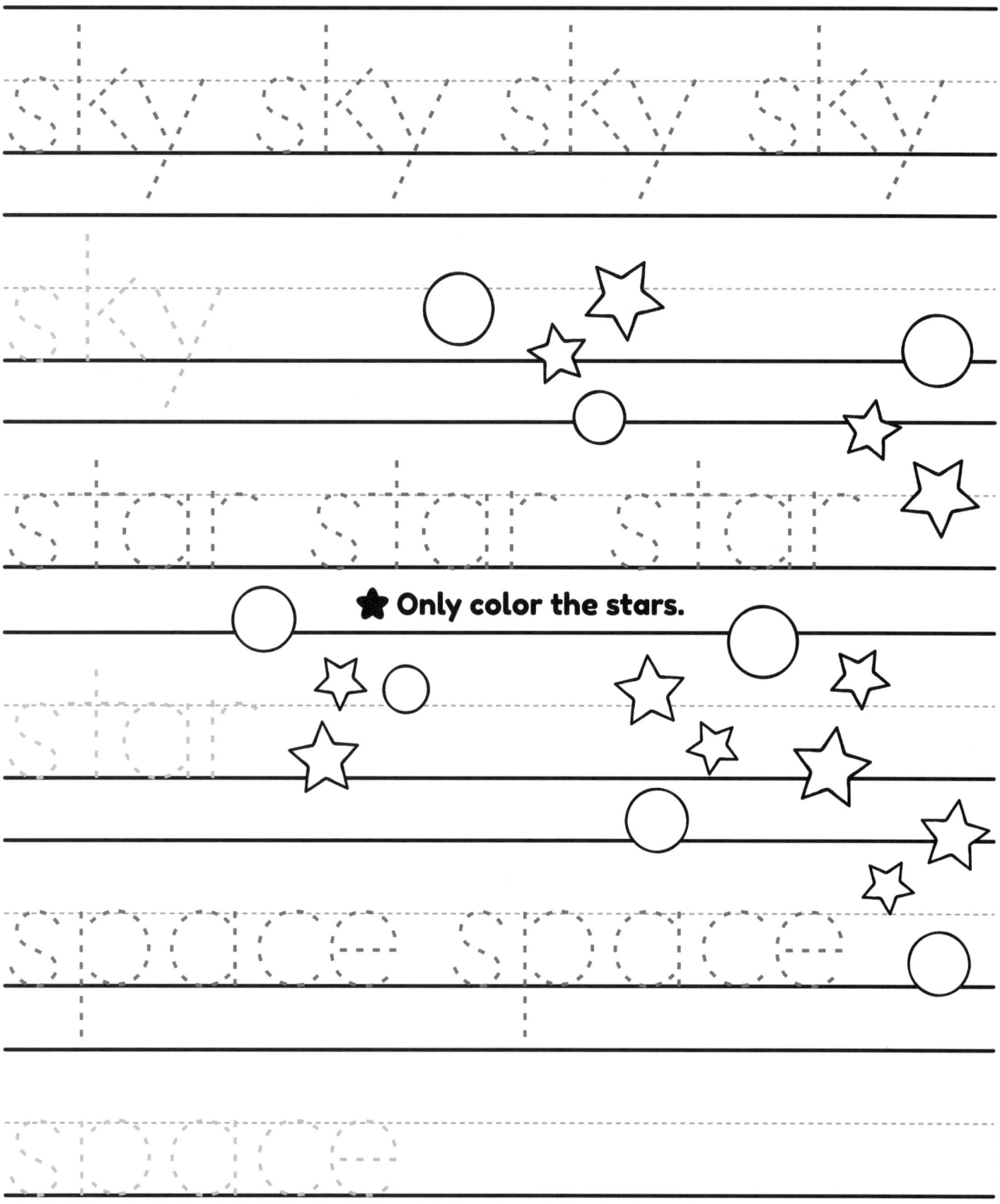
sky sky sky sky
sky
star star star
Only color the stars.
star
space space
space

smile smile

★ **Try one of your own.**

smile

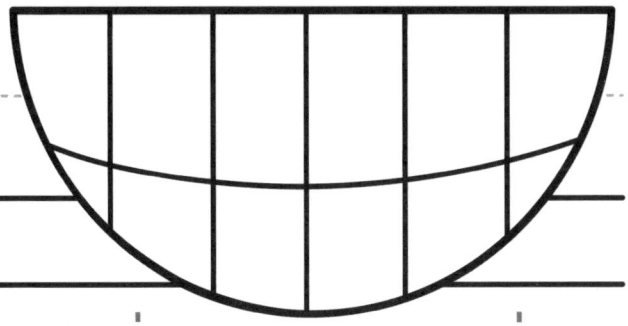

school school

school

Where do squirrels live?

squirrel

squirrel

TRACE, WRITE, AND COLOR!

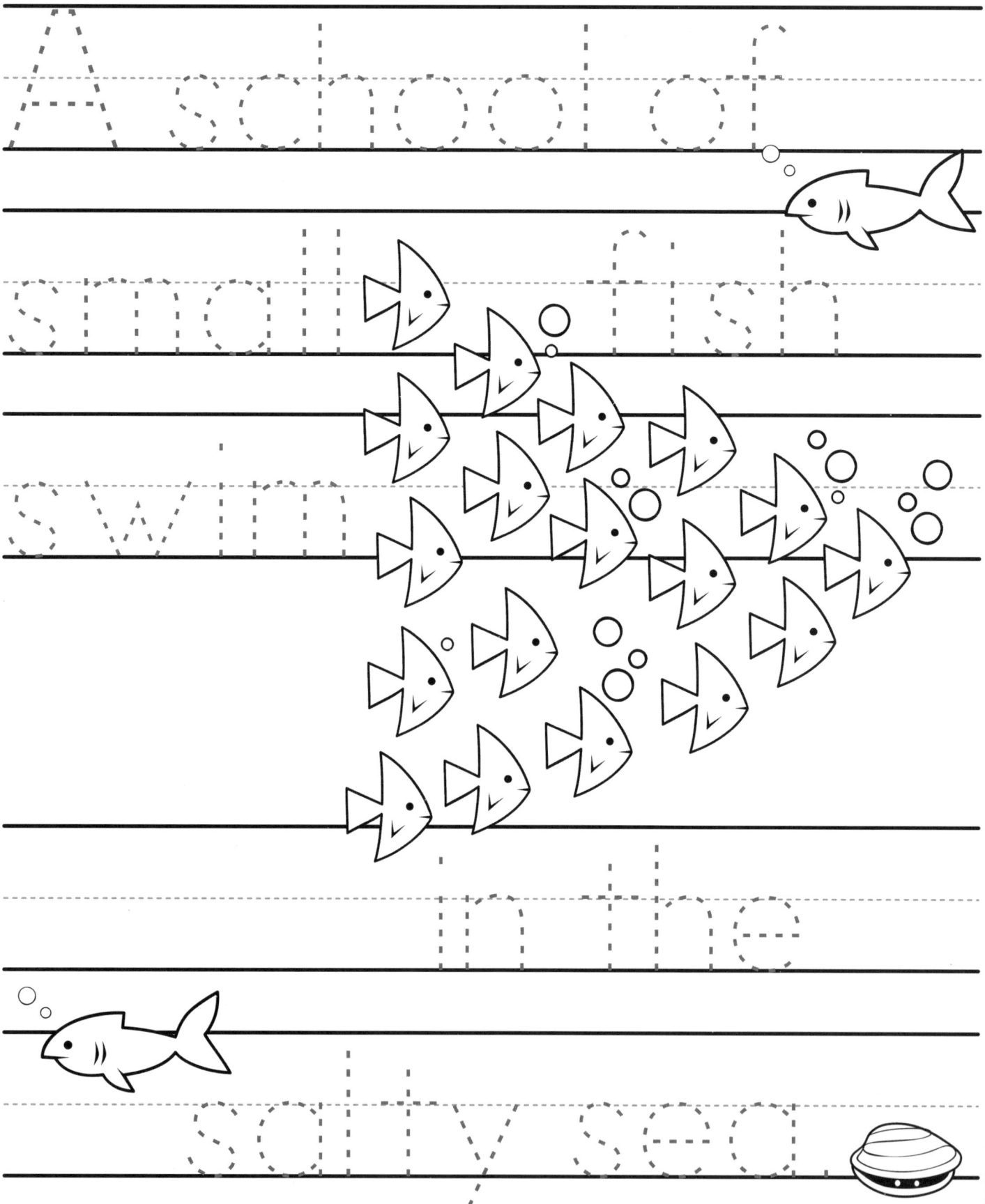

A B C D E F G H I J K L M N O P Q R S **T** U V W X Y Z

CAN YOU WRITE THE LETTERS BY YOURSELF?

WRITE AND LEARN THE SIGHT WORDS.

to to to to to

to

The tallest animal in the world is the giraffe.

tall tall tall

Color it.

tall

ten ten

ten

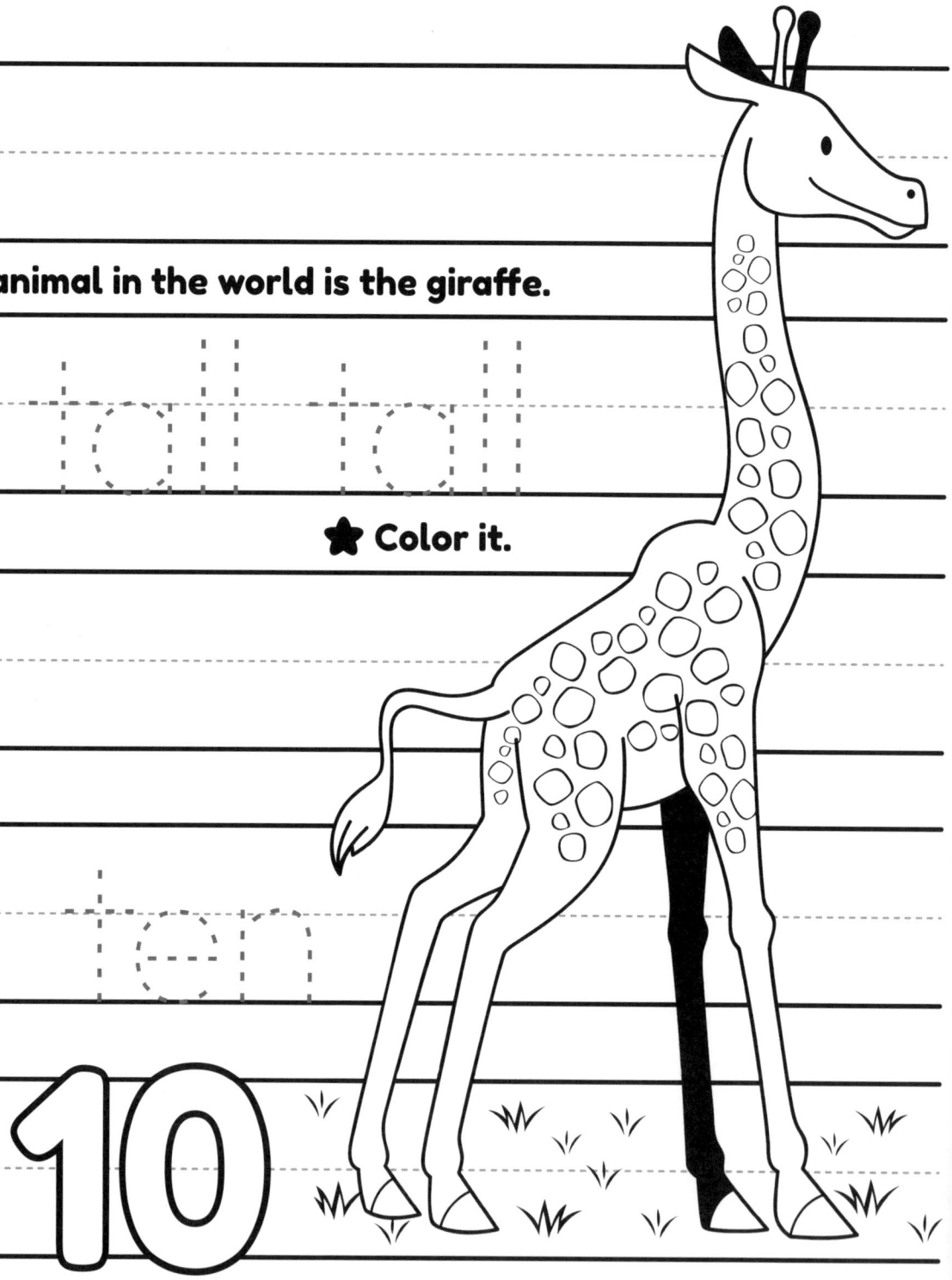

top top top

top

try try try try

try

toe toe toe

How many toes do we have?

toe

tool tool tool

Color the carpenter tools.

tool

tree tree tree

tree

train train

Have you ever seen a train?

train

tomato tomato

★ **It's big and it's juicy. What color is it?**

tomato

turtle turtle

turtle

★ **Color the triangles only.**

triangle

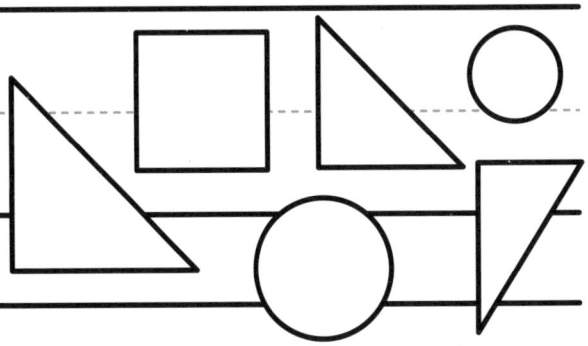

triangle

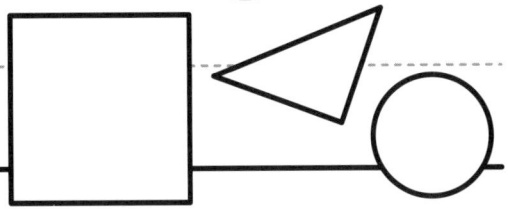

TRACE, WRITE, AND COLOR!

CAN YOU WRITE THE LETTERS BY YOURSELF?

WRITE AND LEARN THE SIGHT WORDS.

US US US US

US

UP UP UP UP

UP

★ Can you draw the balloon going all the way up?

USE USE USE

USE

under under

under

usual usual

usual

uncle

★ **Can you draw your favorite uncle?**

uncle

u u u u u u u u u

u u u u

u n i t e d u n i t e d

What does the U stand for?

u n i t e d

u g l y u g l y u g l y

u g l y

What does the horse need to become a unicorn? Draw it.

unicorn

unicorn

umbrella

What is an umbrella for?

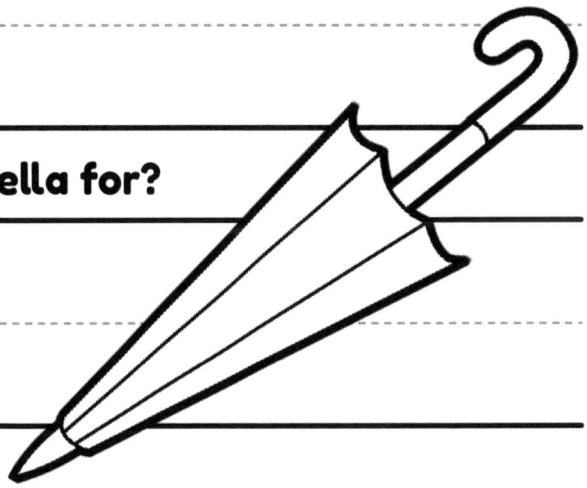

umbrella

understand

understand

★ TRACE, WRITE, AND COLOR!

Come look

at a spider and

see this,

but others

see this.

"There is no ugly."

CAN YOU WRITE THE LETTERS BY YOURSELF?

WRITE AND LEARN THE SIGHT WORDS.

view view view

view

Draw the view from the window.

vase vase

vase

Where do grapes come from?

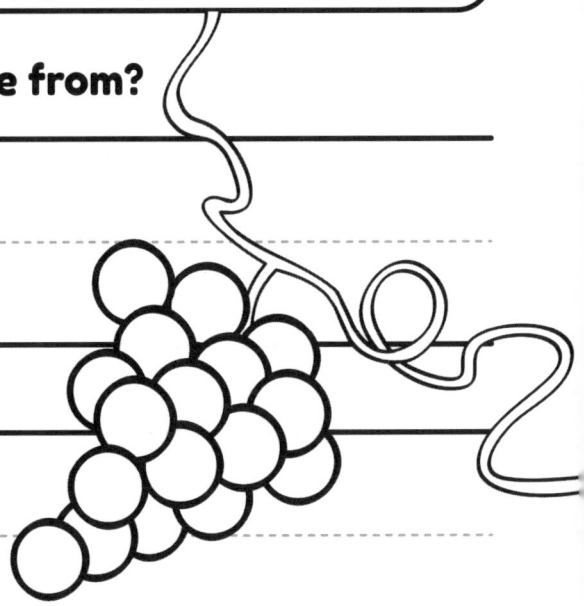

vine vine

vine

very very very

very

vain vain vain

vain

visit visit visit

visit

valley valley

valley

★ **Color the picture of the valley below.**

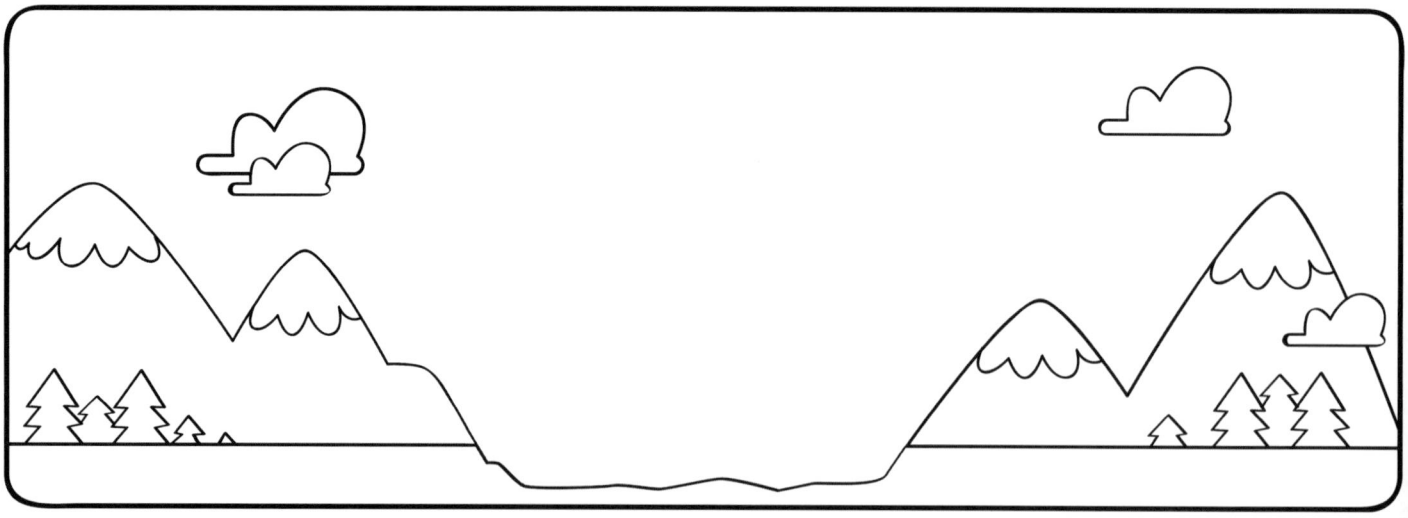

vehicle vehicle

vehicle

Which one isn't a vehicle?

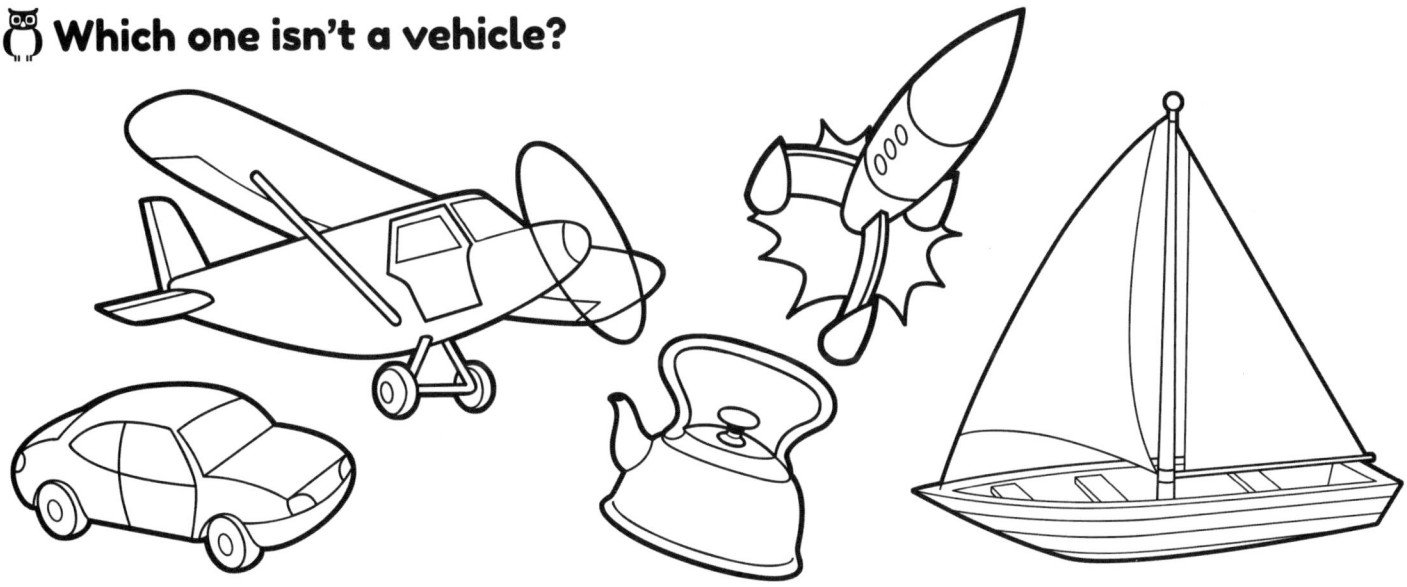

vacation

Where do you like to go?

vacation

★ TRACE, WRITE, AND COLOR!

There are two volcanoes in the valley of dinosaurs.

CAN YOU WRITE THE LETTERS BY YOURSELF?

WRITE AND LEARN THE SIGHT WORDS.

we we we we

we

way way way

way

★ Help her find the way home.

wet wet wet

wet

well well well

well

west west

Where is it from?

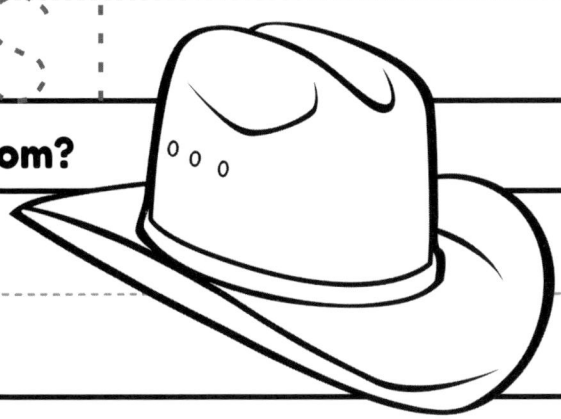

west

wild wild wild

wild

wind wind wind

wind

white white

What color is the snowman?

white

world world

Color the Earth.

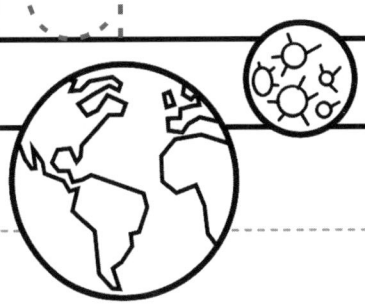

world

write write

What do you use a pencil for?

write

workout workout

workout

TRACE, WRITE, AND COLOR!

White White

the snowman

loves a windy

winter day

CAN YOU WRITE THE LETTERS BY YOURSELF?

CAN YOU WRITE THE LETTERS BY YOURSELF?

CAN YOU WRITE THE LETTERS BY YOURSELF?

WRITE AND LEARN THE SIGHT WORDS.

you you you

you

yes yes yes

yes

★ **Color the egg's yolk only.**

yellow yellow

yellow

★ **Color them yellow.**

yesterday

yesterday

zoo zoo zoo

What animals live there?

zoo

zero zero

What letter does it look like?

zero

zebra

Draw her stripes.

zebra

TRACE, WRITE, AND COLOR!

This young monkey loves to play with his yellow yo-yo at the zoo.

A B C D E F G H I J K L M N O P Q R S T U V W X Y Z

★BONUS ACTIVITY: Color by letter.

A = BLUE
B = GREEN
C = BROWN

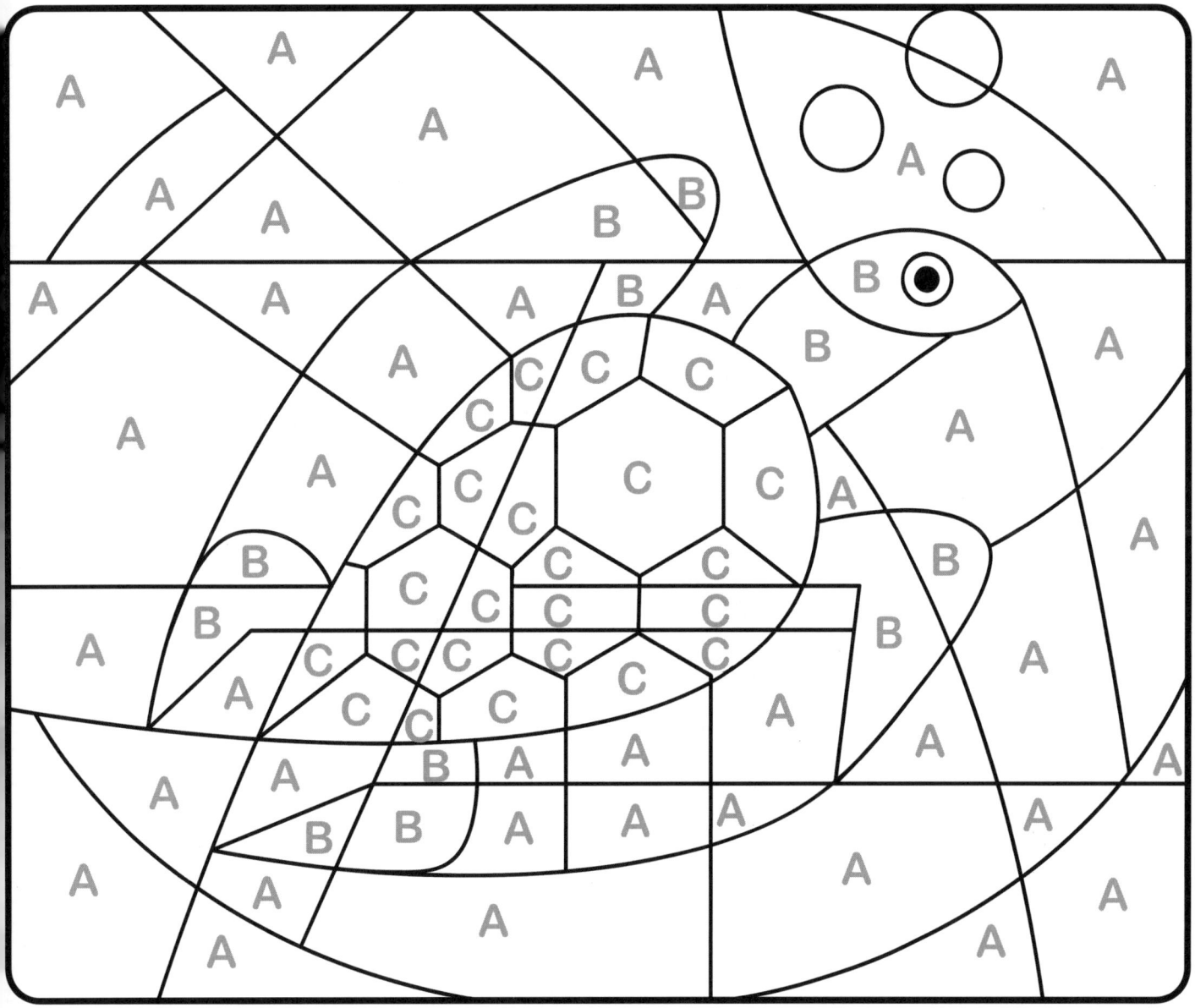

Solution

Turtle

BONUS ACTIVITY: Connect the dots and color.

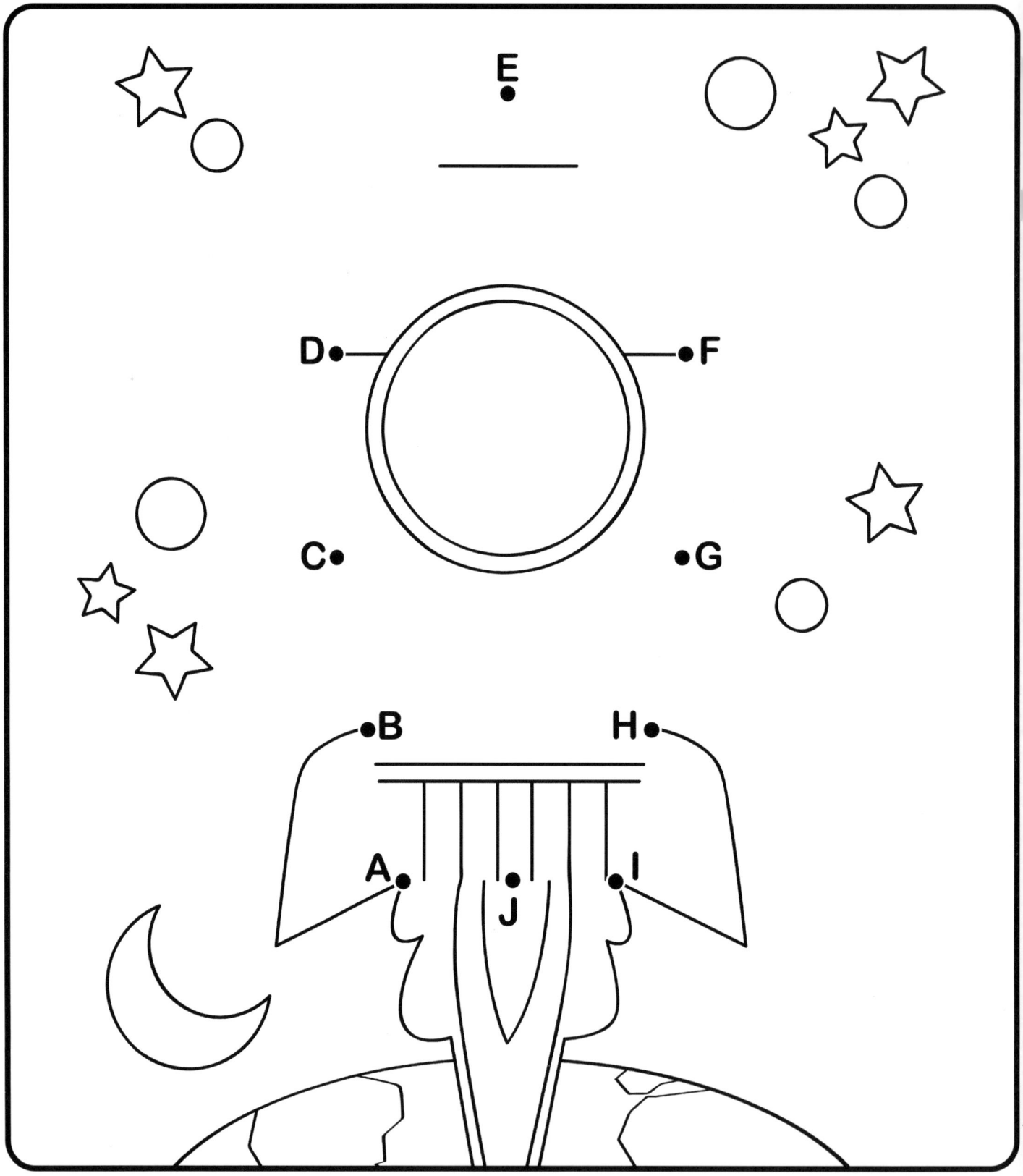

Solution

Rocket

BONUS ACTIVITY: Can you trace each figure with a single stroke?

BONUS ACTIVITY: Find and circle each sight word from the list.

✦ are ✦ ball ✦ ear ✦ get ✦ joy ✦ may ✦ once ✦ pair ✦ sky

BONUS ACTIVITY: Picture crossword.

Solution

a. Bee
b. Rooster
c. Shark
d. Car

★BONUS ACTIVITY: Trace the bowling ball spins to hit the pins.

★BONUS ACTIVITY: Picture crossword.

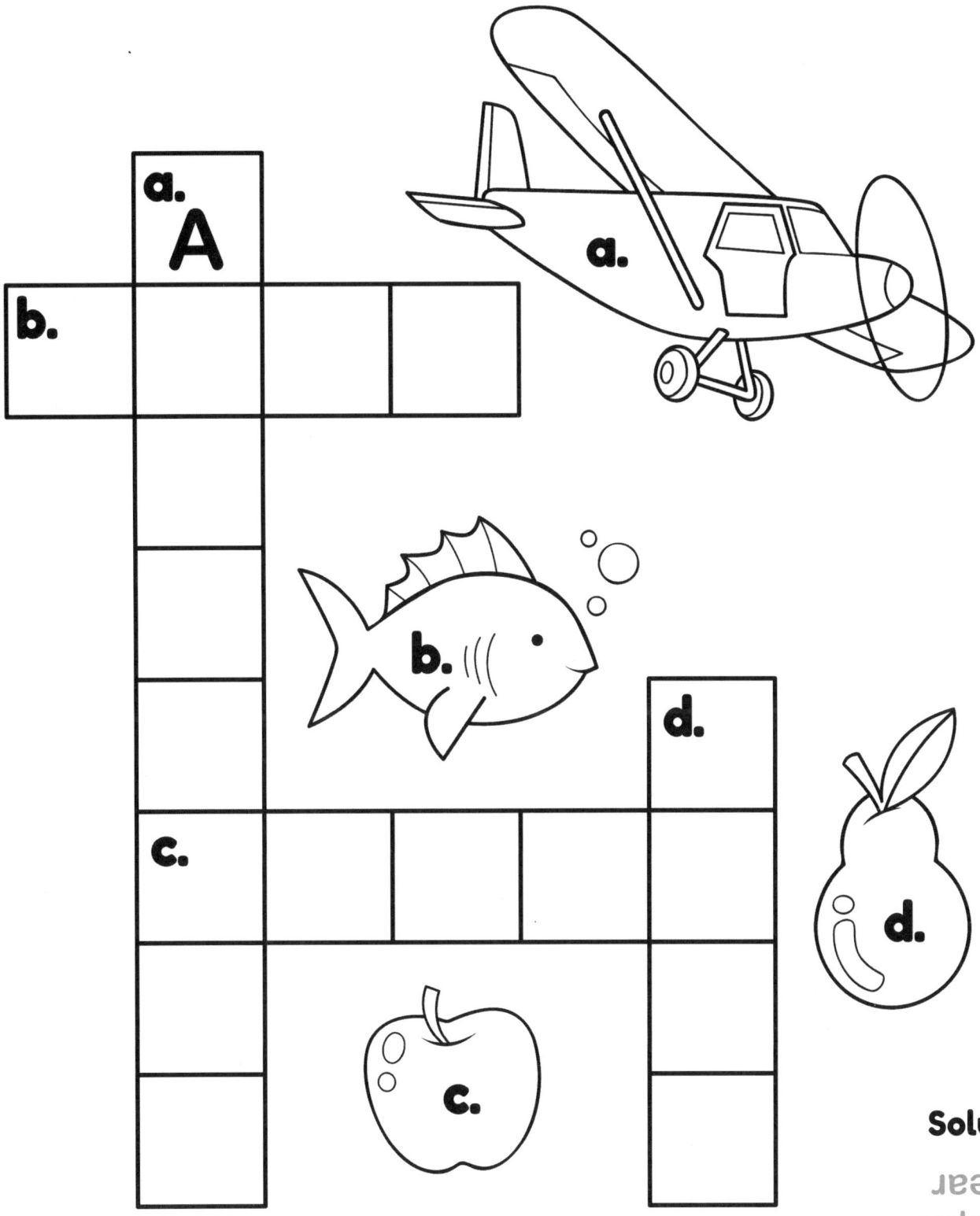

Solution

a. Airplane
b. Fish
c. Apple
d. Pear

★BONUS ACTIVITY: Find the way out of the maze to combine both sight words into one.

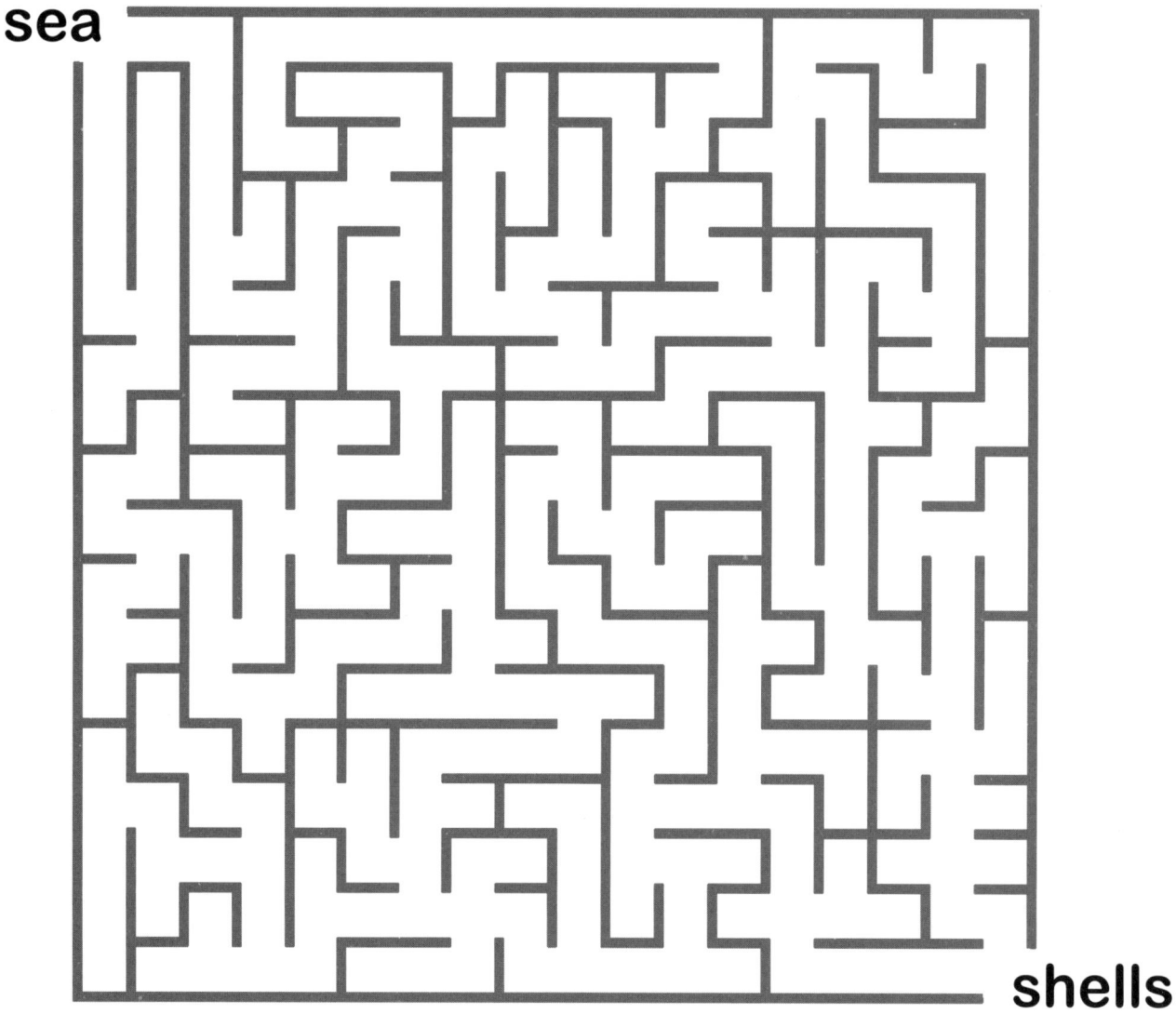

Solution

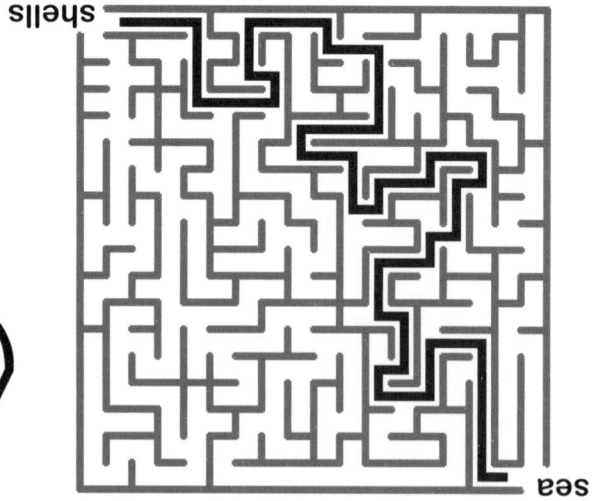

★BONUS ACTIVITY: Complete the tongue twister with the right word.

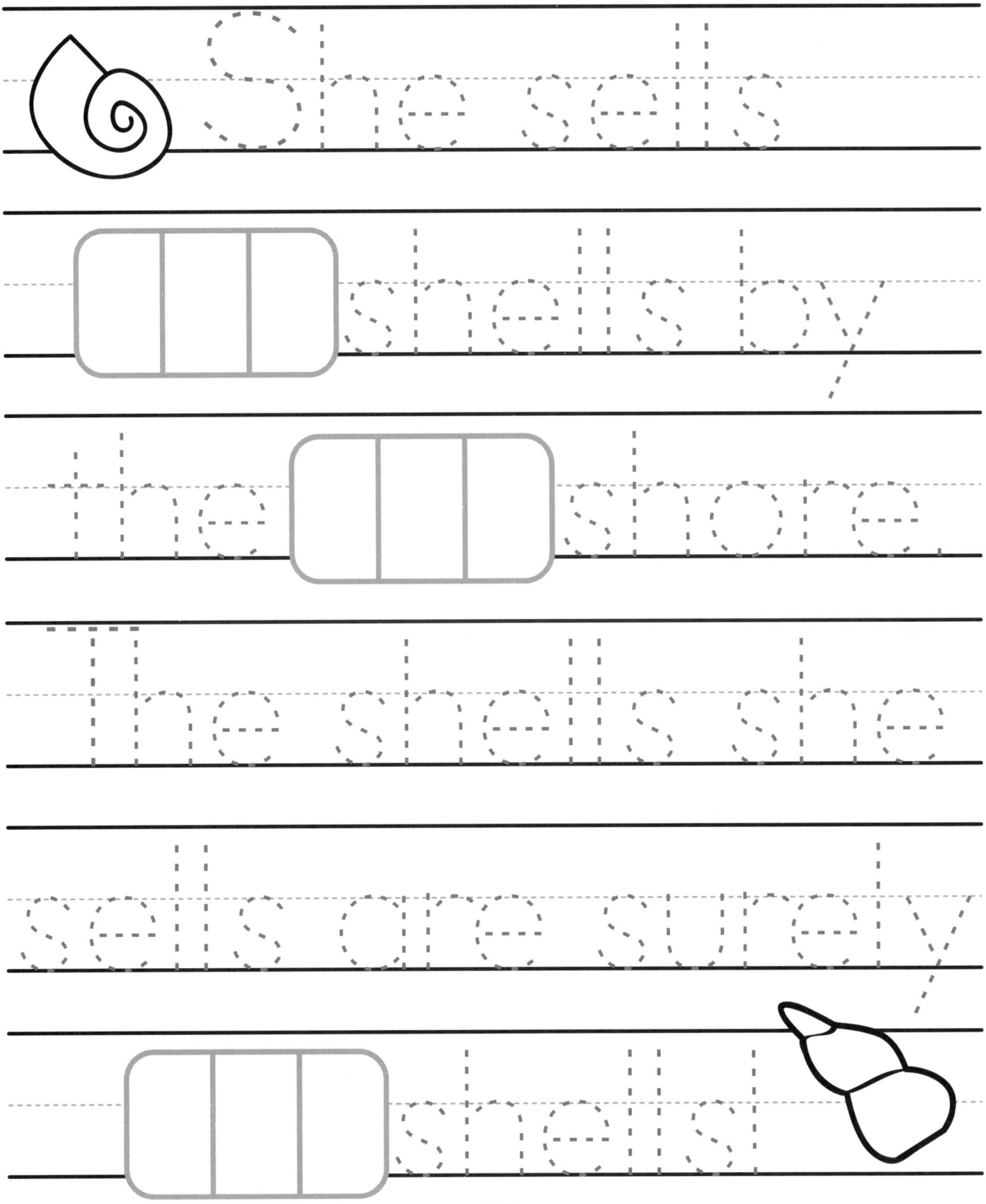

A B C D E F G H I J K L M N O P Q R S T U V W X Y Z

BONUS ACTIVITY: Sight word search.

K	I	N	G	G	O	Y	J	S	M	J
S	T	A	Y	R	A	T	S	U	C	O
V	G	R	M	W	A	I	R	E	I	Y
D	Y	O	E	D	K	S	K	Y	T	K
T	A	U	G	A	C	I	S	F	Y	C
L	Z	N	G	Y	L	J	E	R	W	H
E	O	D	C	A	Z	U	G	U	M	A
L	C	V	V	E	L	W	Y	I	G	S
B	E	E	E	B	W	N	W	T	A	E
U	N	I	T	E	D	S	O	P	M	Q
D	A	W	N	T	R	E	E	W	E	U

Solution

AFTER COMPLETING EACH PAGE, COLOR A STAR TO TRACK HOW MUCH YOU HAVE DONE.

1 2 3 4 5 6 7 8

9 10 11 12 13 14 15 16

17 18 19 20 21 22 23 24

25 26 27 28 29 30 31 32

33 34 35 36 37 38 39 40

41 42 43 44 45 46 47 48

49 50 51 52 53 54 55 56

57 58 59 60 61 62 63 64

65 66 67 68 69 70 71 72

73 74 75 76 77 78 79 80
81 82 83 84 85 86 87 88
89 90 91 92 93 94 95 96
97 98 99 100 101 102 103 104
105 106 107 108 109 110 111 112
113 114 115 116 117 118 119 120
121 122 123 124 125 126 127 128
129 130 131 132 133 134 135 136
137 138 139 140 141 142 143 144
145 146 147 148 149 150 151 152
153 154 155 156

LIST OF ALL SIGHT WORDS INCLUDED IN THIS BOOK

a
above
again
all
always
am
and
answer
ant
apple
are
around
ask
at
aunt
back
ball
be
beans
bee
begin
below
big
bird
blue
boat
both
brown
but
cabbage
cake
can
car
cat
chase
city
close
coffee
color
count
country
dance
dawn
desk
did
dinosaurs
do
doctor
does
dog
doll
draw
duck
each
ear
early
earth
eat
egg
elephant
end
even
evening
every
face
feet
few
find
fish
fly
for
fork
found
freedom
friends
frog
fruit
game
garden
get
gift
giraffe
girls
give
glad
go
grandma
grandmother
grape
grass
green
grew
grow
hair
happily
happy
have
he
hen
her
him
himself
home
honey
horse
hot
how
ice
icecream
idea
if
important
in
inside
into
invent
iron
is
island
it
jacket
jar
jelly
job
join
joy
juice
jump
jungle
just
keep
kettle
key
kick
kind
king
kiss
kitchen
kite
knee
know
last
late
learn
left
less
let
light
like
listen
little
log
long
look
lost
love

man
mane
many
map
may
maze
me
meat
mice
milk
moonlight
morning
mother
mud
music
my
name
nature
near
necktie
need
new
nice
nine
no
now
number
ocean
of
off
on
once
one
open
or
orca
others
owl
page
paint
pair
park
patch
pay
pencil
penguin
people
pig
pigpen
pineapple
pink
plane
play
pour
quack
quarter
queen
quest
question
quick
quiet
quit
quite
quiz
rabbits
radio
rain
rat
reading
real
red
repair
restaurant
right
ring
rock
run
sad
salty
say
school
sea
seashells
seashore
see
seed
seen
shark
sixth
sky
small
smile
snowman
so
some
space
spider
squirrel
star
stay
sun
sure
swim
swimming
tall
ten
the
their
there
these
this
tasty
to
toe
tomato
tool
top
train
tree
triangle
try
turtle
two
ugly
umbrella
uncle
under
understand
unicorn
united
until
up
us
use
usual
vacation
valley
vase
vehicle
very
view
vine
visit
volcanoes
was
way
we
well
west
wet
while
white
wild
wind
windy
winter
with
woman
won't
world
write
yellow
yes
yesterday

yolk
you
young
your
zebra
zero
zoo

ABOUT THE AUTHOR

Diego Jourdan Pereira is an author of puzzle and activity books with a background in illustration, comic-books, and graphic design. In addition to his own volumes for children and adults, he has worked on licensed properties such as Teenage Mutant Ninja Turtles, Transformers, Donald Duck, Grumpy Cat, LEGO, Mars Attacks!, Regular Show, Sesame Street, Star Wars, Toy Story, and WWE, for an international clientele including DC Comics, DC Thomson Media, Dover Publications, IDW Publishing, Skyhorse Publishing, and The Topps Company.

IF YOU LOVED THIS BOOK
DON'T MISS THE
GIANT BOOK OF
GAMES
AND PUZZLES
FOR SMART KIDS
HOURS OF FUN FOR
THE WHOLE FAMILY!